A LAW UNTO THEMSELVES

C. NORTHCOTE PARKINSON

A LAW UNTO THEMSELVES

THEMSELVES

TWELVE PORTRAITS

❧

C. Northcote Parkinson

JOHN MURRAY

Printed in Great Britain for
John Murray, Albemarle Street, London
by Butler & Tanner Ltd, London
and Frome

*FOR
RONALD*

CONTENTS

❧❀☙

ILLUSTRATIONS

❦❦❦

ACKNOWLEDGEMENTS

I am grateful to those who have allowed me to use the quotations in this book, in particular Sir Arthur Bryant; Messrs Faber and Faber, for *Shoot to Kill* by Richard Miers; Messrs William Heinemann, for *Time in the East* by Evan John: and to the following for making it possible to include the illustrations enumerated: Marylin Wailes, 2; Mrs E. J. Simpson, 5 and the example of Evan John's illuminated MS on page 78; the Editor of *Time and Tide*, pages 106/7; The Librarian, Emmanuel College, Cambridge, 3; The Trustees of the National Maritime Museum, 4; The National Portrait Gallery, 6; Radio Times Hulton Picture Library, 7 and 8; Ministry of Culture, Singapore, 9; Mrs Richard Miers, 10; R. S. Martin and Camera Press, 11; *The Guardian*, 12.

PREFACE

Many people feel the urge to write and the books they contemplate are usually, in effect, about themselves. It is the subject, after all, in which each of us is chiefly interested and the subject upon which we can speak with most authority. In so far as I share this autobiographical tendency I have held it on a tight rein, partly because of the inherent difficulty of the task and partly because my career —whether of interest or not to anyone else—is still in progress. A soldier of high rank can describe his victories and end very fairly with a picture of his country home near San Antonio or Tunbridge Wells. An author can seldom write 'Finis' with that sort of assurance. However prolific, he has always just one more book to publish. The considerations, however, which may restrain an author from writing about himself need not deter him from writing about people he has known. This I have tried to do, realising that the result must reflect, in some measure, the sort of person that I am.

Each chapter in this book bears the name of an individual, alive or dead, but has a scope at once wider and narrower than any biography. I write only of the period at which a person was known to me, ignoring much of his career before and since. Nor have I scrupled to introduce other characters into the same chapter and often in a strong supporting role. If I have a precedent for this arbitrary plan it would be found in Sir Harold Nicolson's *Some People*, a classic too brilliant for imitation and yet impossible, of course, to ignore. I have not dared follow him in his masterly blending of fiction with fact, but might have done so had I possessed a tithe of his skill in portraiture or invention. My chapters, howbeit misconceived, deal only with people who are, or were, alive.

Preface

On what principle were my characters chosen? They are, first of all, people whose influence I have to acknowledge. They are not, of necessity, the most distinguished persons I have met; still less those with whom I have been most closely linked in friendship or in some common task. However slight their association with me and over however brief a period, they are among those from whom I have learnt some positive lesson. All the portraits which follow are in some degree favourable and all are of people I am glad to have known. Excluded altogether are those whose conduct it would be folly to imitate. From those too I have learnt in the negative sense by resolving to be as unlike them as possible. These have no place in this book and only a dwindling place in my memory; for that which soils by mere recollection is surely best forgotten. If angry young men are ridiculous, the anger of the elderly is at least as absurd. Men and women are imperfect creatures at best but those I have tried to portray were chosen not for their imperfections but for their merits.

My portraits depict people of varied accomplishments but there is no mathematician or scientist among them. This omission reflects merely my own limitations. Whereas I might have been artist or actor, scholar or journalist, statesman or soldier, nothing (I think) could have made me a physical chemist. In neurology or obstetrics, as in prosthetic dentistry or aerodynamics, my failure would have been humiliating and complete. Scientists I have known and liked but I can neither appraise their abilities nor analyse their success. I could not argue, therefore, that their careers have affected mine. As against that, I have equally omitted all mention of the unscientific people to whom I owe most of all. A man must be deeply influenced in early life by the girls he may know; as later, and still more, by the girl he marries. But these more emotional relationships have been excluded as material for reminiscence, not because they are irrelevant but because the living are entitled to a measure of privacy.

Preface

Consideration for others need not, however, prevent me thanking all those to whom I am more immediately indebted. Some chapters have been corrected by those most nearly concerned or by their widows. I have to thank all those who have taken this trouble and my elder brother, the Rev. R. C. Parkinson, for his finely worded contribution to Chapter 1. I have to thank Mrs Joan K. Neill for typing the manuscript and my publishers for all they have done to give the book its final form. To Ann I owe the peace of mind which makes authorship possible, and to my children I owe such motive as I may have for reminiscence. When all this has been said, I must finally assume responsibility for the book as it stands, as indeed for the author's character in so far as it can be said to emerge. Whether I shall ever become more autobiographical than this remains to be seen and much must depend on the length of life to which I may attain. But should I ever attempt a fuller self-portrait, I would probably insist that, while other people have influenced me up to a point, I have always been, and am likely to remain, a Law unto Myself.

C. NORTHCOTE PARKINSON

Guernsey
20 *December* 1965

1

WILLIAM EDWARD PARKINSON

Duncombe Place was lined by the Scots Greys, mounted, with scarlet jackets and bearskins. Between these two ranks of horsemen, facing inwards, marched the rest of the garrison. There was the blare, thump and clash of each band as it passed, the heavy tread of the marching column and then a moment of relative quiet before the next band struck up in the distance. Scabbards glittered and helmets gleamed, York Minster bells pealed in the background, the crowds filled the pavement and I watched over their heads from a window of what is now the Dean Court Hotel. Although I had no means of knowing this, that Military Sunday in 1914 represented the end, more or less, of the historical period in which I had been born. That was not, however, the thought that occurred to me at the time. Aged four, I was obsessed with a more immediate problem. How, I asked, were the Scots Greys to attend the service? Would they ride into the Minster or would they leave their horses outside? Or weren't they in the mood for religion at all? I put the problem to the maidservant whose grasp prevented me falling out of the window. She assured me that the Scots Greys went to a church of their own, being Presbyterians. Someone else, probably my elder brother (aged eight), told me that the Scots Greys counted as Household Cavalry and would therefore have led the parade had they been part of it. The last band fell silent, the bells ceased their clangour and the crowds dispersed. Inside the cathedral the service began, attended by the dignitaries of York and their wives, my father and mother among them. As for my brother and myself, we

1

witnessed the garrison service from the organ loft, being subsequently taken home by Margaret. She had a walk of perhaps two hundred yards from the Minster to the beginning of High-Petergate. Heading for Bootham Bar, she stopped just short of it, letting herself into a half-timbered and overhanging house on the right; 103, High-Petergate, the house where my childhood was mostly spent.

My previous life had been at Barnard Castle, County Durham, where my father had been Art master of the North Eastern County School. Born at 45, Galgate, I was taken soon afterwards to a new home at The Grove. My first remembered glimpse of the world dates from there and from about 1912. All I could see from the perambulator was a wide street with grass and trees down the centre, and all I wanted was to continue the walk. The person wheeling the perambulator had her own reasons, no doubt, for wanting to go home but whenever she turned back it was my cue, I have been told, to yell. She had devised, therefore, a circular route down one side of the road and back by the other, going through the motions of progress but bringing the perambulator back to its starting point. Of this mean trick I have no recollection at all, my brief picture being isolated from other events, but it may well be that my view of history dates back to this first moment of disillusion. Of the move from Barnard Castle to York I remember little but my brother, being older, remembers more. He recalls what was the greatest thrill of all:

Street lighting in York was still of course done by gas, but the domestic lighting at 103, High-Petergate was electric, and the first we had ever seen. We tried at once to discover what the system would do if we pressed simultaneously the switches on the landing below and those on the landing above which connected with the same bulb. But at night the bedroom which we shared still had its beamed ceiling flooded with gaslight from the lamp in the street outside, and this was extinguished at

2

dawn by means of a pole which was thrust up from below
by a silent man on a bicycle.

Because of its appearance and situation, '103' is photo-
graphed fairly often. It forms part of a building which dates,
essentially, from about 1900; a fact of which the tourist must
normally be unaware. The west front of the Minster is
mostly later still, if it comes to that, but there again the
original concept has been borne in mind. Fronting on
Petergate, a narrow street laid down by the Romans so that
two chariots could pass, '103' backs on Precentor's Court,
where some of the cathedral clergy live or used to live. If
York possessed a cathedral close, '103' would be on the
fringe of it, opening in the one direction on a busy street but
with a backward glance at the Minster. Coming to York in
1913, my father might have chosen a semi-detached house
in the suburbs, Instead, he had chosen this ambiguous
home, flanked by shops and yet suitable—or almost suitable
—for a minor canon. Nor did its ambiguities end there, for
the house acquired, gradually, a social glamour to which it
was entitled neither by position, size nor age. Deans and
Archdeacons were to be seen at the door. Guests would wear
evening dress and there would be the sound of music. On
winter afternoons other visitors might come direct from
hunting with the York and Ainsty. On at least one occasion
I opened a car door which had last been closed by royalty.
The entrance hall, glimpsed from the street, showed the dull
gleam of the weapons hung there—pike and halberd, sabre
and sword. Here were the proper surroundings, one would
say, for a gentleman of rank. And my father looked the
part, being six feet tall, slim and upright, good-looking and
dignified, well-mannered and well-dressed. His previous
home had been in Barnard Castle, County Durham; an
address which tradesmen elsewhere were apt to misunder-
stand. When I first applied for admission to my College I
was invited to give three names for reference and did so,
naming the Archbishop of Canterbury, the Archbishop of

York and the Prime Minister, to all three of whom my father had been known. When he died his friends turned to Chaucer for his epitaph, saying 'He was a verray parfit gentil knight.' And that, in effect, is what he was.

My father died suddenly in 1927, when my brother was at Cambridge and I still at school. A solicitor who had occasion to examine my mother's financial situation at that time looked up from the papers with a startled expression and exclaimed, 'But this is a house of cards!' And so it was, not because my father had squandered his inheritance but because there had been no inheritance for him to squander. He had begun, literally, as a penniless orphan, and whereas many an orphan may die a rich man, having sent his sons to Eton, my father became what he was without making money at all. Our house, '103', had always been a house of cards; a mere figment of the imagination and one we did not even own. My father's position in society was based upon neither birth, education, office, connections or wealth, being mainly in fact a matter of preference. His ancestry was respectable enough, his distant forbears being small gentry in northern Lancashire; but all he inherited from them was a portrait and a family Bible, an oak chest and a bedstead. He was distantly connected by marriage with the noble families of Clive and Northcote. But claims such as these amount to little, being no more than can be made by half the middle-class families of Britain. His education had begun in a Bluecoat School at Chester; finishing admittedly with graduation from the Royal College of Art. He held office merely as Principal of York School of Arts and Crafts. His wife, Rosemary Curnow, was no more than the daughter of an organist who had become headmaster of a private school. And his total income can never have exceeded £750 a year. On this slight foundation he chose to live as a gentleman; but for which choice he might (just possibly) have been more successful as an artist.

How good an artist was he, in fact? In his final examination at the Royal College of Art he took First Class or was graded 'Excellent' in every subject; and there were eighteen of them. He won a silver medal and three bronze medals in national competititions. He exhibited regularly in the Royal Academy and Paris Salon. It is a question, however, whether the uniform excellence of his examination results could be taken as a good omen. Would a future painter of distinction have been equally good at sculpture, and as good again in advanced geometry? Would one destined for eminence as a sculptor have been equally competent in building construction? The results of the really brilliant would be more erratic, surely, or would at least betray some decided preference. I suspect that my father had natural aptitude and great powers of concentration; gifts which would have equally gained him success in another calling. The professional career he had pursued was almost the only one open to a penniless boy of merely primary education, and this is a fact he must have known. What his first choice might have been I can only surmise but he would certainly have succeeded as engineer or architect. For the studio life of Chelsea he was temperamentally unsuited. Many artists of his day were noted for their irregular lives, eccentric dress, socialist leanings and agnostic views. My father, by contrast, was a devout Anglo-Catholic whose morality was never in question, a conservative in politics and one still more conservative in his clothes. He could have passed for a banker and churchwarden and was an obvious choice for the Rotary Club and indeed for the Grand Jury. No artist living could have been less of a bohemian, and this fact was reflected in his testimonials. The Principal of his College Mr J. C. L. Sparkes, spoke of his 'characteristic cool level-headedness' and remarked that 'his eminently gentlemanly manner is an added grace to his ample knowledge and power of business application'. The same note recurs in other letters written on his behalf—'firm but courteous', with 'great business capacity' and 'ability in organisation'. And Professor Lanteri wrote, 'I have always found him a perfect gentleman.' These are not words that anyone would have written about an artist of genius, a Whistler or an Augustus John. One is left with the suspicion that he may have been in the wrong line of business.

Whatever his gift and whatever his limitations, he had the most impressive appearance. My brother makes this clear in the paragraph which follows:

He was handsome and his dress showed awareness of this. Not unlike Sir Henry Irving, he had a good figure for clothes. One photograph shows him wearing a flowing tie but he more often wore a bow to correct the impression made by a rather long head. He had once worn a moustache but was always clean-shaven in later years. He parted his hair in the middle and this suited him. He generally used a walking stick and I cannot recall ever seeing him with one or both hands in his pockets out of doors. One did not often see him reading a book for relaxation. Long after fountain pens had been invented, he was dipping his in ink. He took to using a safety-razor, though, and as an artist he did not disdain the use of a camera. In summer he sometimes wore a cummerbund, a straw hat and even sandals. But he felt the cold and kept the Art School so warm on winter evenings that you had to take your coat off as soon as you had passed the front door. Then, in winter, he wore an overcoat with an astrakhan collar and, over his shoes, spats; while for winter travelling he had a heavy coat that came down nearly to his ankles and a cap with side flaps. I seem not infrequently to have watched him examining writings or drawings under a magnifying glass, which was suspended round his neck with a black silk ribbon. Altogether his appearance impressed people as I think it never failed to please mother.

So writes my elder brother, kindly forbearing to add that the magnifying glass was a substitute for the spectacles which his father refused to wear. In this there was more than a hint of vanity, but he had at least something to be vain about.

William Edward Parkinson

It was assumed in the family that my elder brother would become an architect and that I should become an artist; not, I think, because he was artistically less gifted but because he was academically more promising. I drew and painted, seeming to have no other talent, and this saved me from doing scales on the piano. It may also have saved me from too much parental pressure on the subject of algebra or Latin. I progressed erratically and my only prizes would appear to have been in religious knowledge; in which I have never since recaptured my mid-season form. When I wavered on this question of a career it was because I wanted at one time to become a lawyer. When I gave up the idea it was from a realisation that a barrister needs to have some money and that a solicitor's career can be extremely dull. So I came back to pencil and brush, attended classes and learnt more of the discipline involved. And throughout these years I was essentially my father's pupil, learning much that I have come to value since and more, far more, than I realised at the time. Although my career has led me away from the studio, my father's teaching made an impression. The basic lessons I have never forgotten and they underlie all that I have done since. It would be quite wrong, incidentally, to assume that I lost in boyhood, or have ever lost, my interest in the graphic arts. And whatever aptitude I ever had is still mine, matured even while unexercised. What happened was that other interests, in literature and history, became still more powerful. In so far as I ever became an artist, that is what I still unobtrusively remain.

The first lesson I learnt from my father was how to use my eyes. Confronted by any landscape, by any street or church, he observed both its entirety and its detail. He took in the scene as an arrangement of line and mass, light and shade, colour and tone. Then he went on to study the buildings from a different point of view, guessing their purpose and their date. Last of all he considered any technical problems that might be involved; how had the job been

7

done, or how would he have done it himself? Looking at York Minster, the ordinary tourist absorbs a general impression of grandeur and height. My father, whose eye always went to the roof, took in a precise image of the structure and formed a mental picture of how the timbers were assembled. Perhaps the last drawing he ever did was of a scheme he had conceived for centrally-heating the Chapter House, then for long disused; a scheme in which the pipes would merge as mouldings into the stonework. Practically his last conversation was with Chancellor Austen, old enough to have seen the Duke of Wellington's funeral, and they talked of the cross carried before the Archbishop, which my father maintained had originally been a lantern. His eyes took in anything like this, querying its purpose and assessing its aesthetic merits. From him I derive such powers of observation as I possess; inferior, no doubt, to his and yet subject to the same limitations. And I believe that my life has been better spent because of this ability to see things. It is a skill that scholars often lack and that relatively few people can even understand. To be an artist means to possess, first of all, the gift of vision.

From my father also I learnt something of what he in turn derived from William Morris. Born in 1871 (January 1), W. Edward Parkinson entered the Royal College of Art in 1896. The Pre-Raphaelites were still then providing the chief inspiration. Their movement, supreme since 1848, had admittedly lost something of its momentum. Sir Edward Burne-Jones and William Morris were nearing the end of their lives and G. F. Watts, older than either, was destined to survive them both. Since Morris's involvement with socialism over the period 1888–93, his mission had been partly taken over by Walter Crane, founder of the Arts and Crafts Exhibition Society and Principal, later, of the College to which my father had been admitted. William Morris had preached and his followers had agreed that artist and craftsman are one and the same and that the painter can and should turn from his canvas to design the furniture and

William Edward Parkinson

fabric, the porcelain and pottery, the wallpaper and wainscot of everyday life. It was in this tradition that my father was trained, his knowledge extending to woodcarving, metalwork and enamel. In his time he made everything from communion plate to stained glass windows, from a stage set to a silver casket. Faced by a practical problem, he always knew the answer, and at once.

Walter Crane became Principal of the Royal College of Art in 1898, and it was to him—and through him to William Morris—that my father looked for inspiration. The other artists of the day, Byam Shaw, Maxfield Parrish, Gleeson White and J. J. Shannon, were of much the same school. Domestic architecture was being revived simultaneously by Ernest George and Peto and by M. H. Baillie Scott. My father's friends included Henry Ospovat and Omar Ramsden, with Frederick Taylor as his particular hero. These are not the gods of the present age but the tradition they represented is surely of permanent value. For them a picture was not primarily an expression of the artist's personality. It was a part, rather, of the gracious background against which cultured people could live gracefully. In the creation of the background, architecture, woodwork, metalwork, painting, bookbinding and illustration, ceramics and textiles would all play a part. But the sculptor or artist was first and foremost an honest workman, his task not essentially different from that of the blacksmith or joiner. While one craftsman might make the wrought-iron latch for the door, another might paint the picture of Sir Galahad for the staircase. Some trace of the workman's personality is likely to remain but that is incidental to the main task, the construction of the right background for the given client. The best work has always been the result of the right relationship (however precarious) between client, architect, artist and craftsman. Replace the client by a committee and the balance is lost. Deprive the architect of his craftsmen and his design becomes worthless. Leave the artist to his own desires and the result is lunacy. Give the

9

craftsman's work to a machine and the main product is boredom. All this and more I learnt from my father, and my subsequent experience—as client and committee member, as amateur architect and builder, as decorative artist and carpenter, as bricklayer and painter—has all tended to prove him right.

From my father, finally, I learnt my sense of economy. He had always been and always remained, a relatively poor man; the £250 a year he made in 1901, the £750 he made in 1927 and the £1,500 he might have made today being all in effect the same minimum livelihood for anyone of professional status. Some ingenuity was needed to pass muster socially, on that slender income. My father was more resourceful than most people whose pretensions and means were so sharply contrasted. It was my mother, however, who had the better business sense, as she proved during her widowhood. It never occurred to him to patent the gaspoker, which he invented, or to market effectively the other discoveries he made. The economy he practised was of a different kind and comprehensible only in a special context. In such a life as his he had occasion for the most diverse things to serve the most unexpected purposes. He might want a costume for a model, an extension for the caravan, a suit of armour for theatricals, a sailing ship as Christmas decoration, a top hat for tomorrow's wedding or some additional income to cover his son's college fees. Whatever the need might be, his first thought was to look at what he already had, his last thought to borrow or buy. As if by magic the thing that was there—the scrap metal, the old crate, the torn sack or leaking oil-drum—turned itself into the thing that was wanted. The modern idea of hire-purchase would never, for him, have had the slightest appeal. To borrow something could have frustrated his urge to make the thing desired out of nothing. And, apart from that, the exercise of ingenuity may often serve a variety of purposes. When the old portmanteau is turned into a fireside stool the lumber room is to that extent emptied, the stool is provided

W. E. PARKINSON

in a unique form, the time is usefully occupied that might have been spent in gambling and the children have been taught the value of money. There is a mental satisfaction in recognising that the present encumbrance in the attic can become the umbrella stand in the entrance hall or the property essential to the action of Act III, Scene 2. And provided that no special value is set on the time spent there is an actual saving of money.

Economy in this sense was certainly important to a household such as my parents had established. But, to my father more especially, economy had a further and aesthetic appeal. In every art and craft there is a basic economy of effort. The best painters do no more than is needed to gain the desired effect. The skilled carpenter uses no more force than is required to drive home the nail. The best author says most in fewest words. The householder who knows the art of living will use the same economy, spending no more than is needed in paintwork, no more than he should on wine. He realises that there is no art in extravagance and therefore no interest, but that there is fun in the calculated expenditure which exactly gains our end. It is of this school of economy that I am a graduate and the waste of public money which has characterised our time is for me an offence, above all, against the true art of government. Financially, it has been silly, but aesthetically it has been criminal. I must admit, however, that my father's type of economy could be carried too far. Ingenuity can defeat itself, as his example sometimes proved, and as mine has probably proved more often still. The improvised appliance can be more expensive (in time spent) than its equivalent bought at the ironmongers. But the urge to use material economically seems to survive the occasional setback. The timber left over from roofing the garage has a greater attraction than the complete job. Will it just suffice for a garden seat? It will indeed. But the thing from the shop might (or would it?) prove cheaper in the end.

From my father I learnt, then, to use my eyes, to give art

its true place in life and economy its true place in art. But I chose eventually to study, not art but history. Why? All biographical logic would point to the fact that my Headmaster at St Peter's School, the late Mr S. M. Toyne, was a history specialist and one under whose influence I must have fallen. In point of fact, however, his influence was negligible. In pondering over this circumstance I have come to recognise that his chief failing was, in this context, even more important than mine. Educated himself at Haileybury, the possessor of a good degree and an athletic record at the international and county level, S. M. Toyne had many of the qualifications for headmastership. He was tall, impressive, powerfully built, beetle-browed and eloquent, a good preacher and a good disciplinarian. He looked what he wanted to become, a great headmaster; never seen to better advantage than in cricket flannels or with squash racket in hand. His weakness, as it seemed to me, lay in his vanity. For success in the career he had chosen he needed, besides his other and real gifts, an understanding of the boys he was to inspire and guide. Towards gaining such an insight one must forget oneself, but this he could never entirely do. He could attract the hero-worship of the First XI and the monitors of School House. He could terrify the unruly and idle. But his attempts to understand the boys' capabilities and problems were not always successful. What he saw in their eyes was too often a reflection of himself. His characteristic enthusiasm was for amateur theatricals, in which he always played the lead. Off stage he continued to act his chosen part. He acted well but the result was not always what he expected. The truth is that action and acting are not merely different but opposed. The player is interested in the audience only in so far as they respond to the play and to his own performance. He has the limelight and they the anonymity of darkness. The great headmaster postures on occasion but he trains the spotlight more often on the boys. They are not his audience but the material with which he must work.

William Edward Parkinson

In headmastership my father was superior to S. M. Toyne, being less concerned with himself and therefore, incidentally, more considerate. But, while as I think a finer man, he would not have been the ideal head of an institution less technical than the one he had to control. For whereas Toyne's interest seemed to centre on his own career, too often my father's interest always centred upon the work to be done. And while he took endless pains as a teacher, being consistently patient and kind, he was not a great student of character. He lacked, also, my mother's gift for friendship, our friends being mostly hers rather than his. I question, in fact, whether he had an intimate friend in the world, acceptable as he was to a host of acquaintances. Some four hundred wreaths were piled round his coffin but none, I think, from anyone who knew much of his aspirations, hopes and fears. It was after his death that I was brought into closer touch with S. M. Toyne, in whose form (the History VI) I spent the school year 1927–8 and a part of 1929. It was a period when I might have been deeply influenced by my Headmaster. We were too much aware, however, of each other's shortcomings. Mine were and had always been sufficiently manifest. I had never had any instinct for what a ball would do next. Detesting cricket and too dreamy for success in rugby, I was only mildly successful in cross-country running and rowing. Towards authority I displayed only the 'shallow cynicism' of which the Headmaster complained. If I showed a brisk competence in anything it was in the O.T.C. but that was an unpopular form of achievement. My other characteristics were equally unattractive, ranging from a professed liberalism to a distinction in French (of which I knew nothing) and to the writing of verse—of which I knew less. When in December 1928 the news came of my having gained an open History Exhibition at Emmanuel College, Cambridge, there was a hard frost. So the school was given a half-holiday, for skating. It appeared then that skating was not one of my few accomplishments. There was relief on both sides,

therefore, when I finally left, the Headmaster hoping,
almost audibly, that fate would be kinder to him in
future. And, in one way, it was, for Norman Yardley—
who was to play cricket for England—dawned on his
horizon soon afterwards. It was a fitting climax to his headmastership.

Second influence in my early life was not my Headmaster,
nor any other teacher, but my mother. Born in 1877 and
christened Rose Emily Mary, she was the only daughter in
a family of twelve. John R. Curnow, her father, was of
Cornish descent, a musician and a schoolmaster. Organist of
St John's Church, Chester, he was also headmaster of a
flourishing private school. Curnow used to be a common
name in the vicinity of Penzance, borne mainly by sea-
faring folk, but John's father was the proprietor, I have
been told, of a stage-coach business; one ruined, no doubt,
by the railways. John Curnow was a man of character and
talent, to judge from his photograph, and made what must
have seemed a good marriage with Pamela Coyne, whose
mother had been Pamela Ford, whose uncle was the Vicar
of Llanfoist, whose aunts were the formidable Misses Ford
of Malvern and whose other relatives bore, some of them,
the noble name of Blount. Coyne was the name of the Irish
adventurer who had abducted Pamela Ford from her school;
so nothing was said, apparently, about that side of the
family. It was the Ford ancestry that my grandmother
emphasised, and my mother was sent regularly to stay with
her aunts. Aunt Emily, the elder, Aunt Rozanne, the
younger, were alike in their expression and hairstyle. Tight-
lipped and severe, their hair was parted and drawn tightly
back into a bun at the back. While their guest, my mother
had to undergo the same torture and remembered little else
of what they tried to do with her. The Fords and Blounts
were successful, nevertheless, in giving my grandmother a
sense of her status as a gentlewoman. After her mother's
schoolgirl escapade the Curnow alliance was as much, perhaps, as she could expect, but a Ford (more or less) she

remained, teaching her only daughter to avoid all intimacy with her social inferiors.

If Pamela Curnow was emphatic about her borderline status in society, John Curnow imposed a discipline of his own. Music was his passion and music was, for him, the chief means of education. Given a restless class, his remedy was to make the boys sing, coming back to arithmetic afterwards; the sort of discovery which could nowadays gain someone an educational doctorate. For him a false note was a worse offence than a mistake in the catechism. He was jovial in other respects and had many musical friends, being also in demand as a public speaker. 'Give the man a glass of ale,' he would call when coals or other supplies were delivered at the school, and he was evidently as generous with his children and pupils. How many of his sons reached manhood I have never learnt, nor do I know when he died, save that it must have been in middle age and probably before 1896. Relatively short as his life may have been, he lived long enough to train his daughter as a pianist. She became and remained intensely musical but, being sent to the Queen's School, Chester, she also acquired a love of poetry and drama. At some stage in her upbringing she became a convert to Anglo-Catholicism, in revolt perhaps against the austerities of her mother's background. Ritualism was still a matter of fierce controversy, and her conversion was proof perhaps of a growing independence. She was fair-haired and blue-eyed, quite attractive in youth, but the inheritor of a stubborn chin and resolute mouth. No less than her detested aunts, she had a will of her own. At the age of eighteen (1896) she proclaimed her intention to marry William Edward Parkinson, orphan and artist, with no relatives of consequence and of no education worth mentioning. She was told by her mother (by then possibly a widow) that any such engagement was out of the question, and that she could not marry without her parent's consent. She replied, amidst a stormy scene, that she would wait, in that case, until she came of age; and then marry as planned.

And this is exactly what she did. No relative on either side was present at her wedding in 1899 but she was given away by John Bairstow, who had been her father's closest friend.

Religion was paramount in Rosemary Parkinson's life but she also exemplified the tremendous and sustained force which may derive from a stratified society. Given a sense to begin with of her social consequence, she was grimly resolved to maintain and improve it. I have no idea to this day who the Fords were or what their pretensions can have been, but their niece was left with a sense of mission which underlay some fifty years of disciplined effort. No government or town council can rival a family in persistence and purpose. Hers was vain in that she outlived the society of which she claimed membership. The fact remains, however, that she fairly embodied her husband's family motto *Perseverando et vincit* or 'Dogged does it'. She also emphasised by her example that the basic principle of aristocracy is discipline. The three generations of consistent effort which were the basis, when she was born, of political influence, were linked by an overriding and ruthless purpose. Like many of her school in the past, she had no mercy on herself or anyone else. In her this tendency was powerfully reinforced by the works of Rudyard Kipling, to which she often referred and to which she often looked for inspiration. But whereas an ordinary ambition can induce people to sacrifice their leisure and comfort, the more sustained effort comes from those who feel *entitled* to the status they seek. It is the younger brother's motive, the sense of being dispossessed or deprived, which used to send people on the path of Empire. That the original sense of outrage had often no basis in reason or fact was beside the point. It still provided a source of energy for which our present world offers no substitute. What I learnt from my mother's example was to reject the easy way and the immediate satisfaction. If I showed at any time a sense of purpose I had behind me the knowledge that my mother's resolve was at least as firm.

My mother's idea of worldly success was linked on the one

side with religious devotion and on the other with an alliance of the arts. Wealth she never had or expected but its proper use, she believed, is in the creation of beauty. To her way of thinking the different arts—music, poetry, dancing, form and colour—should be closely knit with each other and with the arts of living—hospitality, courtesy and cookery. On this subject my elder brother writes as follows:

Mother was musical and the daughter of a musician. She was also greatly interested in poetry and in literature generally. Add to this what, to me, is the most important point, that her husband admired her for these interests and was not jealous of them, and there arises the possibility of a household in which the cousinship of the arts may come to seem a natural thing. Now to anyone who may have half-consciously been seeking such a thing for some time, the discovery of its actual existence in a household has a potent fascination. This is what happened in York. There were certainly people who found our household fascinating in Barnard Castle. There were individuals there who saw themselves as fellow-exiles from Athens—or, more probably, the Paris of La Bohème. Our parents had been there and often spoke of it, but in them this interest was made to blend with unhesitating conservatism and strong churchmanship. It was the success of this blending which really constituted their success.

To have made York famous as a centre for the arts was not, perhaps, impracticable, but 1914 was not the ideal year in which to make a start. My early memories include those of a cellar at night with the sound of gunfire, the walls shuddering as the bombs fell near. For the army my father was unsuited by age, by his delicate health and by the disability of a broken elbow. He was a loyal citizen, nevertheless, and eloquent on a method he devised for ascertaining a Zeppelin's height. More important to me was my mother's interest in the Royal Navy; an interest for which there is no very obvious or convincing explanation. York was a seaport once and the home indeed of Robinson Crusoe, but she could have derived little inspiration from its deserted quaysides. As for Chester, her birthplace, its history was very similar, the Mayor being admittedly Admiral of the Dee but with little occasion for hoisting his flag. My mother's forbears came from Penzance, however, and so were presumably pirates; and, apart from that, one of her brothers went to sea as an apprentice in the Gracey Beasly Line. Sailing in the windjammer *Dalgonar* he was present when she caught fire in 1896, being among those complimented afterwards by the Board of Trade. My mother admired the works of 'Bartimeus' to whom and to Kipling she owed what knowledge she had. One result of her interest was the play *Drake's Drum*, which she wrote and produced in 1914–15, the proceeds going to naval welfare funds and a letter of thanks from Sir John Jellicoe, dated on board *Iron Duke*, becoming a treasured possession. Then there were holidays spent at Whitby, with armed trawlers and motor launches in the harbour, convoys in the offing and the occasional sound of distant gunfire. My father took to painting maritime subjects at this time, harbour scenes and fishing craft. One picture I recall represented the German cruiser *Dresden*. I also remember hearing about the raid on Zeebrugge, being shown afterwards the *Royal Iris* and *Royal Daffodil* which had held *Vindictive* against the mole. One way and another I was fully indoctrinated. My drawings were mostly naval and I played eternally with model yachts. The first story I ever wrote—or the first, anyway, which has survived—was a tale of piracy, written when I was about eight. Later came Southey's *Nelson* and Callender's *Naval Side of British History*. I finished my schooldays with a fair outline knowledge of a subject outside the syllabus. By then it might have seemed probable that I should end as a marine artist or as a writer of naval fiction.

While I have ungratefully minimised my debt to the late Mr S. M. Toyne, I should add that other teachers had more success with me, and notably Mr K. H. Rhodes. When that is admitted, however, I would still insist that my earliest

William Edward Parkinson

and most successful teacher was the city itself. I was brought up on a Roman street in the shadow of York Minster. Opposite to where we lived was the house of Sir Thomas Herbert, who held Charles I's cloak on the scaffold. Down the street was the birthplace of Guy Fawkes, christened at our parish church and destined to become my school's most famous old boy. Within a few minutes' walk lay the King's Manor, where a Stuart Parliament met, St Mary's Abbey (objective of a Roundhead assault during the Siege of York), the Treasurer's House, the Guildhall, the Merchant Adventurers' Hall and the city's medieval fortifications. There was history all about me, and I had learnt to use my eyes. I should have been blind indeed had I ignored all that lay almost literally at our door.

And yet it would be an absurd over-simplification to end the matter there. For I was influenced by other authors as well; by Hilaire Belloc, by John Masefield and, above all perhaps, by G. K. Chesterton, whom I was later to meet. It was Belloc, I think, whose example sent me to the battlefield of Marston Moor (1644), where I soon convinced myself that Oliver Cromwell had lied throughout in his account of the battle. I studied the ground with all the military knowledge of a Corporal in the O.T.C. I brought to the tactical problems all the horsemanship I had gleaned from following the York and Ainsty Hunt (on foot and by bicycle). Cycling westwards, however, from York brought me not only to Marston Moor but to Askham Richard. And there I fell under another and potent influence. I could never pass that way, even now, without thinking, first and foremost, of Marylin Wailes.

2

MARYLIN WAILES

The scene is a studio in Hampstead, not far from Keats Grove. It is littered with the cast and the properties of the Noah's Ark touring company, now in the final throes of rehearsal. In one corner a girl and an accompanist are practising a vocal number. Propped behind them is a yellow cow in plywood, with rolling eyes. In the midst of the floor a sword fight is in rehearsal for Oscar Wilde's *Florentine Tragedy*, a sort of one-act Shakespeare. The producer is trying to ensure that the duellists avoid killing each other, and I, the stage-manager and his understudy for this purpose, am wondering how things will work out on a stage of half the size, such as we may well encounter on tour. Sitting on the rolled-up carpet, which has been thrust aside, two characters in costume as the Walrus and the Carpenter are discussing the business of their act. Opposite them the assistant stage-manager is painting a backcloth while another corner is given over to the colouring of posters and the repair of a spinning wheel. One side, however, of the studio is of glass and reveals a rockery which hides all but the sunset sky. In the midst of the tumult and confusion and almost unnoticed there enters up-stage a diplomatist in immaculate evening dress. He might well have passed as the conjurer but he is actually a real diplomatist, the guest of the principal dancer. He has been asked to supper and his hostess will not let him starve. Bounding forward with that vitality which makes everyone else seem relatively paralysed, she drags him off to a tiny kitchen. The two of them presently reappear to sit in the rockery, each with a kipper on a plate. The picture needed only a title; 'The Yellow Cow' perhaps, or 'Duel to the Death'; and it would have to be dated '1930'.

The principal dancer was Marylin Wailes, and her astonishing life, as so far unfolded, was a slightly more complex version of A. P. Herbert's *Tantivy Towers*. That opera turns, as everyone knows, on the conflict between Chelsea and the Shires. 'Let no one take *me* for an artist,' sings the heroine's brother, 'for Yorkshire's the shire I reside in. And there I have fun with the smartest, with Huntin' and Shootin' and Ridin'.' Her dilemma was whether to live in Chelsea or hunt with the Yaffle. Marylin's dilemma had been the same but with her alternatives going to extremes outside the scope of opera. Her choice was not merely one of marriage, as between a baritone and a Master of Fox-hounds. Her marriages were to be incidental to a career in which she was more artistic than the artists and far horsier than the horsemen. Over an active life, which still continues under full pressure, she has left all her contemporaries dumbfounded and aghast. Faced with a choice as between stage and stable, studio and concert hall, Leicester-shire and Little Venice, she hesitated not an instant but chose—the lot. When I first knew Marylin she was Dorothy Wailes-Fairbairn of Askham Richard, the strikingly beautiful and athletic daughter of an apparently typical Yorkshire landowner. In point of fact he was less typical than he seemed, having begun life as a cowboy. Apart from that, however, he had a large mansion (now a reformatory) with vast stables, ballroom and indoor swimming pool. He was in a position to entertain royalty and did so. His daughters were in a position to marry into other landown-ing families and did so, the younger being known to this day as among the best horsewomen in England. But Dorothy, the elder, painted pictures when not actually riding. This brought her into contact with my father and so with my mother, whose closest friend she became. They talked of poetry and music and art and finally, with still greater enthusiasm, of dancing. In 1921–2 they founded a school of Greek and Imaginative Dancing, which met at the School of Arts and Crafts. The first public display was held in the grounds of the Archbishop's Palace on June the 26th, 1922. The most obvious result of this effort was that Dorothy, the leader and teacher, ended as a professional dancer, and the inventor, indeed, of a system of choreography. She was still well known in the hunting field, where she made history in Yorkshire by riding astride, but Greek dancing tended to happen at a different time of year. When her first marriage broke up, she went on the stage as Marylin Wailes. She was dancing professionally in 1930 and was known throughout Europe. This phase, which included the Noah's Ark episode, ended with her second marriage, which brought her back to the hunting field, this time near Market Harborough.

But Marylin, now Dorothy Morton, was not content to hunt, train, breed and sell horses, exceptional as her knowledge was. Being fluent in French, she talked with Versailles experts on 'haut école' and reached the conclusion that galloping over fields and jumping hedges need not be the final achievement in equitation. Back in the 17th century, before the hedges had been planted and before war itself had become impossibly regimental, the experts had trained their horses for individual and knightly combat. Something of this tradition survived in Austria and France. It had been the speciality of the Duke of Newcastle (1592–1676), whose gifts were so sadly wasted at the Battle of Marston Moor. Why should this higher form of equitation be left to foreigners? Why not revive it in England, as something more interesting than a mere point-to-point? No sooner said than done. Known now as 'Dressage' the art was reintroduced and has become the basis of competitive horsemanship as displayed each year at Badminton. Mrs Morton, as she then was, visited Vienna in 1936 and talked fluent German with the pundits of the Spanish School; where, but for gastric influenza, I should have been with her.

Marylin Wailes

After World War II Marylin Wailes, as she had again become, established herself in London, this time as a musician. But just as her horsemanship had been of the most esoteric kind, so now was her music. She played the bass recorder in a consort of unusual and learned people, performing publicly or on television. She also collected ancient musical instruments and learned how to play them —instruments of medieval or renascence pattern of which the mere names (let alone the technique) had been more or less forgotten. For some years her time was divided between performance and teaching, but then the pattern changed. She became a musicologist and plunged into research, unearthing the scores of 17th-century composers whose work had been overlooked. Martin Pearson was her discovery and she wrote learnedly about the period in which he lived. She was well known at the British Museum in those days and added a great deal to our knowledge of 17th-century music. After making a substantial contribution to knowledge, she changed direction once more. She decided to become a painter for the second time and live for parts of each year in Catalonia. This she now does, attempting to speak Castilian and Catalan and exhibiting at galleries in Spain and London. Heaven knows what she will do next but it will be brilliantly done, whatever it is, and she will be recognised at once as a leading exponent if not indeed as the chief authority in whatever the subject may be. Marylin's varied and powerful talent is a force of nature, defying all likelihood, comparison or time.

Marylin was the leading spirit of a group of people who frequented '103' between about 1920 and 1927. These friends included several who were still army officers, stationed at Fulford Barracks. Geoffrey Dearmer, the poet, was one of these but the others were more typical of the cavalry regiments to which they belonged. Dean Foxley Norris had artistic leanings and so had Brigadier-General Mends. There were musicians as well, and then, in 1925, came Dorothy Holmes-Gore as lead in the touring company of G. Bernard Shaw's *St Joan*. She became a constant visitor and close friend and, when she married Evan John Simpson (the playwright and producer) he too joined the circle. But among all these cultivated people Marylin was always the source of inspiration; partly through sheer vitality, partly because she alone could talk with equal enthusiasm and knowledge about everything from saddlery to satire, from counterpoint to crayon. Whether in pursuit of a quotation or a fox, Marylin was always in at the kill. It was from her that many of my early ideas derive and when I showed some tendency to fall in love with her niece, that intelligent girl married someone else, observing (with considerable insight) that my admiration was not directed towards her as she existed but at the younger version of Marylin which I believed her to be. She may perhaps have understood me better at that time than I understood myself.

What did I learn, meanwhile, from Marylin? I learnt first of all to reconcile the life of the countryside with the life of the city. My own upbringing had been within a few yards of the cathedral, the theatre, the library and market place. The medieval fortifications had offered me and my fox terrier what has been rightly described as the best before-breakfast-walk in England. My holidays were divided between the Yorkshire coast and the Yorkshire moors. I might ordinarily have dismissed the arable countryside as fit only for yokels. I might have concluded, further, that one has to choose between the easels and the weasels, between the graces and the grouse. It was Marylin who taught me that no such choice need be made and that the same person can be stockbreeder and soldier, painter and poet. The art of life, as she has lived it, is to be equally at home in different worlds, never an exile and never a guest. In her philosophy, however, the arts, whether of drawing or dressage, are supreme. She did not go on, as an Elizabethan might have done, to study diplomacy and politics, finance, theology and war. But if art was her subject, she took it in the very broadest sense, her mastery extending to food and wine,

the art of travel and the art of life. To Marylin nearly everything is fun.

Without Marylin I should not have realised—or not have
realised so soon—the importance of breeding. Much of the
talk in recent years has been about environment as opposed
to heredity. And it is manifest that, to people brought up in
suburbs, environment must seem all important; for heredity
is something they have had little occasion to observe. They
rarely see each other's grandparents or grandchildren, and
seldom know anybody for more than a decade. In the country
there is an intense interest in heredity by contrast, as applied first of all to horses, cattle, dogs and cats, and so by in-
ference to human beings. The inherited qualities are at once
more obvious with a shorter life cycle, and of more obvious
importance. All thoroughbred racehorses derive from the
Eclipse, Herod and Matchem sire lines, practically all classic
winners coming from what is virtually the same stock, and
three-quarters of the leading stallions being descendants of
Gainsborough, Phalaris or Swynford. The study of lineage
first applied to horses, camels and dogs, later to poultry and
pigs, has been transferred with less certainty to human
beings. We are not as confident, to begin with, about the
human qualities we think desirable. As against that, all
aristocratic practice tends to ensure that the ablest men
have children by the prettiest girls or else by daughters of
men whose ability is comparable. By this alternation, half-
consciously pursued, the family's mental and physical
qualities are improved, a later generation being able to
accomplish what their ancestors could not have dared
attempt. It was from Marylin, initially, that I took my
notion of breeding as applied to mankind.

But aristocracy means more than that. Its second principle is that the son can start, most unfairly, at the point on
the ladder to which his father had climbed, and to com-
plaints about unequal opportunity the answer is complete
and final. It cannot be done in any other way. For while the
individual ascent from log cabin to White House may be

just physically possible, the climber is usually too old and exhausted on arrival to be of the slightest use. The problem of leadership on the highest level is that of combining experience with youth. The democratic practice is to combine inexperience with age, which plainly will not do. It was in Marylin that I saw the result of the opposite or aristocratic process. Her actual place in the cultural history of England is smaller perhaps than it should have been, her efforts being so dispersed, but she could never have done what she did without starting from a relatively high level. Her experience in dressage would have been impossible for someone whose early years had been spent in making the money with which to buy horses when middle-aged. One can learn to ride in later life but one can hardly begin from there to revolutionise the art as hitherto known. For all to start equal may be theoretically attractive but it is something for which life is too short.

My mother's literary tastes ran to poetry and drama, and so I think did Marylin's. My own, in early years, were influenced chiefly by John Masefield and G. K. Chesterton. Masefield gave direction to my boyhood ideas about the countryside and the sea, about fox-hunting and sailing ships. From him again, in the long run at least, I derived my standards of English prose. Masefield's descriptive and narrative writing is far beyond my imitation but it is the sort of thing I should like to have written had I possessed the talent. 'Santa Barbara lies far to leeward, with a coast facing to the north and east. It is the richest of the sugar countries. . . .' We can well believe it. In four pages Masefield makes this imaginary land more real than most shown in the atlas, a few deft phrases bringing it to life. His countrysides and seaports, his mansions and rectories are more real, perhaps, than his leading characters, but his poet's skill makes the story inimitable, each taut sentence hinting at so much more than it actually says. He would have been our greatest naval historian had he not become our Poet Laureate. His was the prose upon which I sought

MARYLIN WAILES (*left*)

to model my earlier works and I believe to this day that I could have found no better guide to the practice of literature.

But Masefield, great as he is, can do no more than describe what he has seen or imagined. He is no philosopher or critic of his time. He accepts, as well he might, the Victorian ideals at their best, reserving his condemnation for those who rebel against properly constituted authority. While as willing to suppress the anarchist, I had no comparable faith in Parliament. Being something of a rebel by nature (as my headmaster had complained) I was loyal only to the Monarchy and could see no particular merit in Cabinet or Commons. As compared with some authors I admired, I was growing up, moreover, at a later period. Those holding high office lacked the prestige of success. Attempting little, they were achieving less. Nor has the passage of time added anything much to their reputation. Whether Conservative or Labour, they mostly seemed then what they seem more obviously in retrospect, a second-rate collection of the ineffectual and dishonest. My parents being conservative and my elder brother (at that time) a socialist, I should perhaps in any case have called myself a liberal. But G. K. Chesterton made me a liberal of that extreme group called distributist, a minority within a dwindling minority, a sect within a dwindling sect. Led by G. K. C. himself and inspired by Hilaire Belloc, it was fatally weakened from the outset by its apparent link with Catholicism. It was nevertheless the party to which I belonged in those days and for which, on occasion, I was prepared to speak. It fairly represented what was left of liberalism in a world which essentially had no place for it.

But why did I take Chesterton, not Belloc, for my example? Why prefer the journalist to the historian? Some of Belloc's historical prose was unequalled in his day and is never likely to be bettered now, but Belloc failed somehow to attract. This may have been due, in fact, to some unspoken queries about his loyalty. His family background (atheist and nonconformist) allowed him to be either French or English. He chose to be English but revealed for the rest of his life an uncertainty as to whether he had chosen aright. Was his allegiance to the Crown or to some concept of a Catholic Christendom? For me that concept had no reality and, incidentally, no appeal. The ghastly parody staged by Mussolini and Pétain was the end, eventually, of what had never been more than a sentimental News from Nowhere. Belloc had few supporters, however, even when his case seemed more plausible. It is true that G. K. Chesterton's views were much the same but he was at once English and likeable. He could join with Belloc in caricaturing politics, finance and high society, but one felt that his love was for England and London, for Fleet Street and Notting Hill. He may have liked foreigners but he never dreamt of becoming one. He was a part of the English scene.

Between leaving school and going to college I spent some months as assistant in a tutoring establishment at Beaconsfield. I remember little of what I taught or to whom, but my hours of leisure were spent in learning to play tennis and learning to ride. I remember attending Henley Regatta, too, but any such frivolity was overshadowed in importance by my meeting with G. K. Chesterton himself. He lived at Beaconsfield in those days, at a new house called Top Meadow, suburban in its situation but equipped with a small theatre. It was on the stage of the theatre that he worked, and there he was when I arrived. I had come with an introduction from somebody but soon no doubt revealed my distributist views, claiming to be a disciple in my own right. He was very kind, as he must have been to everyone, and told me of his annoyance with the local authorities. They were proposing to fill in a pond at a road junction, oblivious of its picturesque merits. One could imagine it (he said) as the sort of pond in which an old gentleman's body might be found floating. I hoped politely that this argument would prevail and mentioned a little later that I had been visiting the nearby village of Jordans with its almost oppressive atmosphere of Quaker enlightenment. G. K. C. told me then that he had been invited once to address the Jordans Literary Society, the agreed title of his speech being 'William Penn'. Thinking it over, he resolved to praise Penn at length but for the wrong reasons. Penn, as he knew, had been not only a Quaker but the friend (rather oddly) of Charles II. G. K. C. proposed to emphasise this friendship and explain that, with the help of more people like Penn, the Stuarts might have been still on the throne. 'Unfortunately,' he sighed, 'I boasted too widely of my intention. The word got round and I received a last-minute request from the secretary—'Would I talk, instead, on Charles Dickens?' Being the kindly man he always was, he agreed to this and spoke accordingly. . . . We met on at least one other occasion and exchanged letters on some political theme, but I never saw him again after that. I still think of him, however, as one of the most original thinkers of his day.

Although he was a poet of eminence, Chesterton's strength lay in his essays. I never greatly admired his novels, partly because his characters are usually dwarfed by his ideas and partly because his style, for that length, becomes tedious. But there was nobody living who could make as valuable a comment on practically any subject that might arise. He could be riotously funny but the joke always had a foundation of philosophic truth. He always went back to first principles, argued from them with strictest logic, reached a sensible but unexpected conclusion and then put it forward as a laughable paradox. Readers were to laugh first at an absurdity, realise afterwards that it contained a profound truth, and finally remember the truth by remembering the joke. I was afterwards to learn, as a teacher, that humour is invaluable but only so long as it sugars the pill. The joke which people will memorise, must be inseparable from the lesson which they might otherwise forget. The joke that is merely incidental serves only to distract and should be avoided. This I was to learn by experience. What I learnt directly from Chesterton was that a sane and logical argument can be disguised in a joke and so become twice as effective. I realised also that the sagest counsel and the wildest mirth can have exactly the same origin, both deriving from a sense of proportion. The absurdity of the wrong answer can be appreciated only by the person who knows what the right answer should be. In Chesterton's essays the wit and wisdom derive from the same source and reveal the same quality of mind. But the joke requires more thought than the grave pronouncement, embodying as it does a double process, the perception of a truth and the recognition of an error. More than that, it is the absurdity of the false which points the way to what is true. Having read somewhere that the Demand creates the Supply, we realise not only that this is often untrue but that the converse is far more helpful—the Supply quite obviously creates the Demand. If I have any claim to be thought either a philosopher or a humorist, I owe both qualities—and still more their conjunction—to G. K. Chesterton. His death in 1936 left the world a poorer, duller and much crazier place.

G. K. Chesterton was, at this stage in my life, an appropriate hero, for he had hesitated, as I was to hesitate, between literature and art. He was known, indeed, as an illustrator even after becoming far better known as an author. Nor had my own decision been taken when I went to college. I could even then have elected to do research after graduation in the history of art, and my background was still more artistic than academic. I might end, I supposed, as a schoolmaster but the people by whom I had been most deeply influenced had not been graduates at all. I did not go to Cambridge with any idea of making the university my career. Its appeal for me was aesthetic, romantic and social. And if history was my chosen subject, I did as yet not see myself as an historian. I had a great love for York, which remains close to my idea of what a city should be. I had a feeling for local history, but as much again for local architecture and landscape. And the effect of my father's death in 1927 had, in one way, intensified my interest in the arts.

Marylin Wailes

For I began then to make money as painter and toymaker, earning enough eventually to pay my own school fees. As author I developed more slowly, my first published article appearing in the *Yorkshire Herald* of October the 26th, 1927. In it I described an Officers' Training Corps Field Day near Levisham, making quite a spirited account of what had been (for me) a rather uneventful battle. My authorship was instantly detected and deplored by the Headmaster, whose notions of style were more pedestrian. His own account (if he wrote one) would not, I suspect, have been as readable as mine.

At the time, then, of my brief stage-managerial experience, I was still undecided as between authorship and painting, and painting, as I knew, is perhaps the most satisfying of the arts. The canvas, whether large or small, reduces the world to a manageable size. Within that square or oblong we can create the order and beauty for which we crave. The composer has some comparable satisfaction but has to rely upon others for the performance. The painter, by contrast, has everything to hand and relies upon nobody. Confined only by the nature of the subject and the limitations of the material, he has absolute power over the scene he has chosen to depict. On the stage we have to cope with a complex inter-relationship of persons and purposes—the dramatist and producer, the players and the audience all contributing to the success or failure of any one performance. So diverse are the elements one wonders how the thing is even possible. But the painter rules serenely in the world of his imagining, enjoying a sense of achievement which the musician (to judge from his expression) sees eternally beyond his reach. It was with great reluctance, therefore, that I relinquished my first career. Nor have I ever ceased to believe that I may, some day, return to it; very much as Marylin has done.

Should I ever paint again, however, it will be, I suspect, for a limited purpose. For the final lesson I learnt from Marylin Wailes—a lesson confirmed since by experience—

is that one should never look back. It has been my fortune to work and move in different types of society in various parts of the world. After each change of surroundings my practice has been to make the transition abrupt and complete, wasting no time on recrimination or sentiment, writing to nobody and never seeking to return. For, after all, what alternative is there? If we look back too much, there is no time for anything else. And time, as we grow older, is the main shortage. The days and years are not long enough for all that one would like to accomplish. Like Marylin, I have had no occasion for 'pastimes'. So far from playing cards or billiards, I have never so much as attempted to solve a crossword puzzle. Passing the time has never been my difficulty, and life is too full of real problems to leave me leisure for the synthetic kind. Each day ends, as it is, with the thought of how little has been done of all that is to do. There is no time for letters and Christmas cards as well.

There might seem to be an element of self-contradiction in the theories I have just outlined. Were I to revert some day to the studio—as Marylin is tending to do—could I not be breaking my rule and hers? I do not think that this is so. To come back full-circle to the starting point is not the same thing as to falter, hesitate, and retrace one's steps. For the art to which one returns, after a lifetime of experience, will never be the same. The later phase will be so different as to be scarcely recognisable. It may seem strange that an art should mature when not practised, but it certainly does. There is an initial difficulty, perhaps, over the hand's unsteadiness; for a painter works to a high degree of precision. With the recovery, however, of manual dexterity, the former artist enters a new phase of work, a 'later manner' sharply different from the first. He is not turning back but pressing on. But while the result will be very different his contentment may be the same, for he will have turned from a world he cannot organise to a world he can put in order. Within the limits of the canvas he can find a substitute for all that life has failed to yield. There, if nowhere else, he can make the world of his vision coincide, at least seemingly, with the world of fact.

My stay with the Noah's Ark touring company symbolised the choice I had to make. I could even then have turned back to the studio or stage. But Cambridge was asserting its influence. It was there, above all, that I came under the spell of Edward Welbourne, then my Tutor but later Master of Emmanuel. He was for years a legendary figure in Cambridge with his caustic wit and sudden insight, his quick assessment of personality and his deep love for the College. A university's best gift to the scholar is the contact it offers with first-class minds; and especially with the minds of those who are still alive. Welbourne was then and always tremendously alive. Generations have been quickened by his influence and the College itself raised tremendously in its reputation. I followed my elder brother to Emmanuel, the choice being to that extent accidental, but have never since wished it could have been otherwise. Granted that I am what my school, my college and regiment have made me, I am more especially Welbourne's pupil; a fact which has emphasised my rebel tendency. For Welbourne was never a characteristic historian of the Cambridge school. He was a very learned man but never in that orthodox way which leads smoothly to the Athenaeum. Too much of an individualist for that well-trodden path, he has produced pupils who are mostly individual too.

3

EDWARD WELBOURNE

Edward Welbourne, recently retired from the Mastership of Emmanuel College, was the chief influence in my life at Cambridge; nor has he ceased to influence me since. He was surely among the ablest men that Cambridge has produced in the 20th century. In mere force of intellect he can have had few rivals in his generation, but there was something in his character—and more in his war service—which denied him a still greater success in a far bigger world. Of fairly humble origin, he had wanted in early life to be a farmer, but lacked the capital with which to begin. He reached Cambridge with a knowledge of the countryside but of little else, aware from the beginning that war would interrupt whatever he tried to do. He served with distinction, but the Armistice of 1918 brought him back to Emmanuel with an open leg wound, a well-earned Military Cross, his health impaired and his illusions gone. His trouble thenceforward was insomnia, the result of pain, lessening through the years but never absent. With farming ruled out, his second inclination was to read for the Bar, and this he did. He came to realise, however, that a successful career at the Bar demands, first and foremost, the ability to work at top speed for ten years at a stretch. Welbourne no longer had that sort of stamina. The rising barrister must not fall sick, but how could a wounded man be sure of that? So when the opportunity came to remain in the College he took it, doubting then and since whether he had chosen aright but grateful to be offered some certainty for the future. Even the frictions of academic life might have proved too much for him

EDWARD WELBOURNE *(centre)*

as a bachelor, but he had married an eminently pleasant and sensible lady of Scots origin whose support made all the difference. He also acquired a home outside Cambridge where his children were brought up, as he had been, in the country. There, in a moated farmhouse called Granhams, he had somewhere to which he could withdraw. For the rest of his active career, travels apart, he moved between two fixed points; his book-lined rooms in College and his home at Shelford, the latter at least symbolising the career of his first choice. He was never a near neighbour of those who ruled the university and his reputation among them was rather that of cynic and rebel.

History was his subject and he proved his knowledge at the outset by winning the Thirlwall and Gladstone Prizes, receiving the Seeley Medal, and publishing two good books, the last in 1920. There were no further publications, for he had settled down to a college life which absorbed all his energy. He had thenceforward to make his influence felt through his pupils. For a man who had suffered so much and who slept so little, he did prodigies of work. He gave lectures and tutorials, sat on Boards and Committees and served at one time as Proctor. As Fellow, as Tutor, as Senior Tutor, and finally as Master, he did a great work for the College; work little remembered, however, outside its walls. His more lasting influence was as a conversationalist and it is as such that his pupils will recall him. Many of his observations were recorded at the time or repeated afterwards and some are current still. There is, however, an obvious danger in quoting him now, as I mean to do. He was, to begin with, a complex character and I recorded or recall his remarks only to the extent that I understood and applauded them. I probably missed as much as I absorbed and misunderstood as much again of what I thought to have learnt. It is obvious, moreover, that the views he held in 1929–37—or the theories, rather, which he propounded then for the love of argument—are not of necessity his final conclusions or later beliefs. He talked sometimes for the effect (as of surprise), leaving his friends to decide for themselves whether to take him seriously or not. And while he was, like Dr Johnson, the most stimulating of thinkers, his more positive opinions were to be inferred mainly from the list of things and ideas he was known to deplore. Making short work of his pupils' cherished beliefs, he left some values unscathed; values which they might discover, some of them, on their own. Never the ablest of his pupils, I may well be among those who understood least of his positive teaching. I cannot record what message he had for the world but only the effect that he had (perhaps unintentionally) on me. As a biographer I may have failed, therefore, except in literal accuracy, and can claim only the merit of concentrating my efforts on a single subject. I have never been tempted to play Boswell to anyone else.

'When the habit has grown up among Historians to say one thing, it takes a bold man,' said Welbourne, 'to take the other side.' Such boldness he had, and not merely in confuting the scholars. The Establishment was his target for many years before the word was used. Historically, he argued, the gentleman was a soldier turned thief, the thief turned magistrate, and each magistrate in league with the rest. 'Do you realise,' he would ask (in about 1930), 'that there are a hundred and four Etonians in the present Parliament? It will end at the lamp-post.' 'We have reached and passed the limit of direct taxation. But there are as many foxhounds as ever!' Nor would he allow that the gentleman had retained much value in war, for most of the English officers at Waterloo had risen from the ranks. 'It was only afterwards when all the immediate prospect of fighting was over, that the English officer began to be a gentleman again; and only long after that did Sandhurst close the profession to men of ability.' Would one dare conclude that the Victorian N.C.O. must have been good? Not a bit of it: 'All sergeants get promoted to that rank by knowing how to flatter their officers.' Perhaps wisdom lies more, then, in society as a whole? Far from that, 'English Society is moved by three great forces; Protestantism, Asceticism (or teetotalism) and Over-Exercise to counter-balance over-eating.' Would things be better if people were better informed? No such thing, because 'Facts have no influence on our minds. If they did, we should go mad.' Perhaps, then, it is the solid folk who matter, the tradesmen who save, the farmers who follow the plough? Wrong again, because 'Saving is brought about by ignorance of how to spend,' and 'Most of our saving consists in compelling the next generation to do without something,' and 'Farmers never believe each other!' Is it to the poor then, that we should look for patterns of virtue? That least of all, for 'About ten per cent of the population can be classed as imbecile.' Are other countries any better? Hardly that, for 'A strong minority of Germans like war for its own sake—or at any rate until they have had some of it.' As for the U.S.A., the American schools form a peg on which to hang something should they ever be able to decide what. 'This is characteristic of mankind—only about one per-cent of our opportunities are ever used.'

Many of Welbourne's chance observations might be made the subject for a book; but not one, apparently, of his own composition. His efforts and affections all went, rather, into his College, which stands now higher in repute than at any time since the 17th century. Chief cause of its success has been Welbourne's work as Tutor, Senior Tutor and Master; his work, above all, in choosing the right candidates for admission. 'The don's skill today,' he said once, 'is in telling the difference between teachable and unteachable undergraduates; not as easy as when the Parson had a family of ten. He used to know that Parson's sons are always all right but that Postman's sons need choosing.' Uncannily accurate and swift in assessment, Welbourne thinks more of the family than the school. He is sceptical indeed about the whole business of teaching. 'Education, he said once, 'is a fiction. It is merely the acquiring of the capacity to live in the society of people similarly educated.' More than that, 'Education is a handicap; it fills the mind with wrong notions before the opportunity comes to see facts.' He was nevertheless among the best teachers and stood still higher among the best administrators, matching a rigid honesty with a robust common sense. 'There is no greater mistake,' he would say, 'than paying too much for things. Pay more than you need and the thing you pay for will be worse, not better. Do the thing too lavishly and you may get something bigger than you wanted it; or, alternatively, you may get nothing.' He had a critical eye for plumbing and plans, for sewers and sinks. The College's hygienic kitchen dates from his Mastership but he admitted that the cooking would never be the same again. 'It's the bacteria that give the taste.'

It was said of Welbourne by his pupil and my contemporary, H. S. Offler, now Professor at Durham, that his wildness in talk was balanced by a commendable caution in policy. That is true, but it is fair to ask which will be the longer remembered, the administrator or the conversationalist? Welbourne had a theory or an epigram ready on any topic and at any time. And he had the art of expressing himself in what Jeremy Bentham described as 'the language of plain strong sense'. Whether sitting in his study or walking across the paddock, whether in the Fellow's Parlour or meeting a friend in Petty Cury, he would deliver himself of thoughts like these: 'The best way to be silent is to talk the whole time about something else.' 'All quarrels are family quarrels.' 'Always screw in a corkscrew as far as it will go—the man who made it knew how long a cork is.' 'It is always best to begin with the easiest job.' 'Meat is a town food because it is the only kind of food which will walk into the town.' 'People have only started using the word "development" quite recently. It came in with the camera.' 'Where it is warmer it is also smellier.' 'Constipation comes from doing a clerk's work and eating as much as a farm-labourer would like to eat if he got the chance.' 'You can't catch salmon with a rod—you catch them in a sort of weir made of rushes; or nowadays you let the fishing to a foreigner and give him a rod to stop him catching anything.' 'Honey is dear because bees sting and most people are afraid of them.' 'The great open spaces have been populated through people going there in the belief that they provide lots of food and no work, and never having enough money to get home.' 'The Pole went to America because everyone in Europe hated him.' 'The best way to prevent stealing is to give the thief what he wants before he steals it.' 'When a new thing is invented, some men will pay more for it than it is worth, because it is new; other men will not buy it at all unless you give it to them—and for exactly the same reason.'

With this keen observation and comment went a number of prejudices. First, there was a dislike of the pompous— 'The man who uses his judgement is doing the opposite of using his intelligence.' 'High finance consists in sitting round using your judgement until someone suddenly shouts "Good God, the stuff has gone!" Then you are off the gold-standard.' With this went a healthy distrust of the philanthropist, the do-gooder. Characteristic was his opinion of 'University Extension' or 'Extra-Mural' activities: 'I have always said the thing is an imposture. Pupils of mine have done it; and they all tell me the same thing. If you make your lectures anything like work, nobody will come. So you can do one of two things. You can fake the register or you can make your lectures rival the cinema by turning them into a cinema show. The whole thing is a waste of money which ought to be spent in encouraging real students. The origin of it was the desire, probably, to keep the working classes quiet; the desire to educate them just so long as that didn't mean sitting down to dinner with them at Trinity; the desire, above all, to keep them out of Cambridge.'

It was first my privilege to have the set of rooms at Emmanuel that had belonged first to Richard Farmer (1735–97), Fellow, Tutor, Doctor of Divinity, Master of the College and ultimately Vice-Chancellor of the University. He was a friend of Samuel Johnson and I was enough of a Johnsonian to think with awe that the great man must have been a visitor to the rooms that were temporarily mine. In so far as I played Boswell—as many another pupil must have done—it was because Welbourne had something in common with Johnson. He had the same downright vigour in conversation, the same love of argument, and even some of the same half-serious prejudices. To regard Welbourne as anti-intellectual would be absurd but he preferred common sense to the more arid and pretentious kinds of scholarship. The same might have been said of Johnson, who was a very learned man indeed. But was Welbourne, like Johnson, an opponent of the Scots? His pupils might sometimes have been tempted to think so, as when he would observe that 'The Scotsman got to know about money through never having any. That is what ruined Charles I. He knew that the pound paid him in taxes was only five shillings. So they put him in his place—with the axe.' While this sort of remark may imply no actual criticism, the general tone of the conclusion might be thought lacking in grief. But here his deeds were more significant than his words. For he not only married a Scotswoman but had Jock Wallace as perhaps his closest friend in the College, and Hunter-Blair as Senior Tutor during his Mastership. In the light of his known friendships the Scots have no cause to resent any jests he may have uttered at their expense.

In point of fact, this unserious prejudice sprang from his attitude towards people in general. He was never very willing to credit anybody with an opinion based on mere reason. Considering statesmen and scholars of distinction, he used the same analysis as he used to apply to candidates for an entrance scholarship. After glancing at the application form and the examination scripts, and after talking for two minutes with the lad himself, Welbourne would reach his final conclusion in a matter of seconds. 'A boy of non-conformist family, probably bullied by his mother, badly taught at Wheresit Grammar School (where some VI Form master has been reading the *New Statesman* to the class), he has barely average ability and will achieve a lower

Edward Welbourne

Second in the Tripos.' That was that, and the judgement was one of uncanny accuracy in nearly every case. Cambridge may have had, and may have, a score, of other men who can do the same trick as swiftly. But Welbourne's cool assessment was not reserved merely for the young. It was never enough for him that a certain theory should have been advanced by a certain author. He wanted to know *why*; and the answer always went back to the author's family background and origin. Was he brought up on a Welsh farm or near a Northumberland coalpit? Were his parents refugees from Poland or shopkeepers in Dublin? Did he go to a Quaker school or was he brought up in Bermondsey? Essential to his attitude and constantly reaffirmed in his talk was the realisation that historians and economists are themselves a part of the scene they are trying to depict; not academically detached but emotionally involved. That history is being written from a certain angle was to him an historical fact. That economists uphold a certain theory was again, for him, a result mainly of their upbringing—certainly not a stage in intellectual progress.

It is this habit of mind which made him seem more prejudiced than he was. Discussing Ramsay MacDonald or Charles I, the central fact, for Welbourne, was that both were Scotsmen; heir perhaps to certain virtues and prone, perhaps, to certain mistakes. No talk about Pioneers of Socialism or Martyrs for Religion would distract him from the facts which he thought basic. Like any other East Anglian countryman looking at a cow, he wanted to know where it came from. There is a sense in which this sort of analysis could be overdone but he was certainly right in believing that the current trend is too much the other way. People who are brought up in London suburbs never see each other's grandparents—or grandchildren, for that matter—and have no idea of what heredity means. They are ready, therefore, to accept theories about the influence of schools, books and radio programmes. No one brought up in a farmyard would make that sort of mistake. For

Welbourne a tendency to gamble was as obviously inherited among men as a male strain may be inherited among pigs.

For individual historians, therefore, as for history itself, his respect was apt to be scant: 'I have no reverence whatever for the past,' he would say (and no more, he might have added, for the present); 'Professor Bury had one emotion comprehensible to man, if only one; and that was anger!' 'Ramsay Muir is a second-rate fellow.' 'Morley is a fraud.' As for Tawney, 'I cannot read three pages of Tawney's *Acquisitive Society* without wanting to vomit.' In his attitude towards economists he could verge, by contrast, on actual intolerance. But here again he was aware of their background: 'Economics began to be studied here when 18th-century dons, necessarily in holy orders, sat down and said, "How can I reconcile it with my conscience to take £200 a year from the College as dividend when my remote predecessors had only £10 a year? Am I not the worst of men, violating my oath, cheating the poor scholar?" And then he sat down and quieted his conscience by proving that his predecessors' £10 bought him as much beer as did his own £200, which revealed the change in the value of money. But he was wrong in thinking himself no better off than his remote predecessors. He *was* better off; for he proceeded to build Georgian Cambridge.' Nor would Welbourne admit that the accepted theorists were the best: 'Defoe was a much better economist than Adam Smith. He knew more about it. He went bankrupt three times. He had lost money lots of ways. And in his book the good nonconformist Robinson Crusoe no sooner found his island than he got Friday to do all the work for him.' Or, as Welbourne remarked on another occasion, 'When people talk of the fluidity of labour they mean slavery; labour is not fluid—but slaves are.' From Petty and Defoe he traced a decline in economic ability. 'Ricardo knew more about money than Marshall because he had more of it. He had a million while Marshall only had £10,000; so he knew just about a hundred times as much about it.' ' "Free Trade," the English economists would say, *standing on English Railway Platforms* "is our defence against Monopoly!" '

'When you read the great economists' remarks on population, remember that few of them had children—Marx was an exception and *he* only had daughters.' As for the economists of his own generation, Welbourne would complain that they too were mostly unmarried or childless and sterile, therefore, in other ways. 'Marshall's economics were informed with desire for the improvement of mankind. He wanted the poor to be not quite so poor. He wanted them to read instructive books. He wanted to get them out of the pub, and he wanted no less ardently to get them out of the church.' 'The economist generalises from conditions as they were fifty years ago.' 'Textbooks on economics are apt to be about, apparently, nothing at all.' 'I differ from Professor Pigou in not believing in abnormal phenomena which must not be thought of.' His advice to those taking examinations was to use the fashionable words. ' "Trend" is the word our economists like. "Natural" is the word they used to like and "Divine" is the word they liked before that. . . . Use the word "Elasticity" with a proper reverence. It should be handled like the miracle of the Mass.'

If there was something less than reverence in Welbourne's attitude towards the historians and economists, he came to see that these are almost respectable when compared with some other teachers. Lowest in intellectual status —before the advent of the educationalisers—were the protagonists of Political Thought; and among these pitiable creatures, the lowest form of animal life, Sir Ernest Barker was in the abyss beyond the abyss. 'I suppose,' Welbourne used to sigh, 'it is best to assume that, when a man *says* he understands a subject, he does really see something in it. And so one must try to admit that Professor Barker knows what he is talking about. But *I* can't make anything of his stuff; it conveys nothing whatever to my mind. And the books he recommends are just as meaningless.' On the subject of political theorists and actual politicians Welbourne could well conclude in the words of Jeremy Bentham: 'There are two classes of writer to whom the public is very little obliged; those who pretend to say something and in effect say nothing; and those who say something but say not what they think.'

Here then is our picture of the stricken field, with the corpses piled high and the educationalisers at the bottom of the heap. Who remains alive and what battle-cry is still to be heard? What was the positive side of Welbourne's teaching? What did his pupils actually learn? He never had any message for fools. With the more intelligent and responsive, however, his success used to be brilliant. What his success was with me I am not to know but I can still remember the method he used. My first essay in my first term was on (shall we say?) the Franks. It began something like this:

> To understand the nature of the Barbarian invasions which led to the collapse of the Western Empire, it is necessary to understand the nature of any invasion or conquest. With few exceptions, all invasions on a large scale have been not isolated, startling and unforeseen events so much as violent culminations of longer term processes. The Norman Conquest of England did not really take place in 1066; Norman costume and Norman architecture had begun to come into England long before that time. The Normans themselves, in fact, had begun to arrive before that. The first man of consequence the Norman troops met on their landing was a Norman; and the army which faced them at Hastings was armed in exactly the same fashion as the French followers of the Duke of Normandy—

'How DO YOU KNOW?' came Welbourne's question like a pistol shot, and I groped desperately for my authorities. My theory collapsed in so far as the Norman Conquest was concerned, and, as for the Franks, I never actually reached them. Nothing more was heard of my essay, which was possibly just as well, and Welbourne passed on to something else. Whatever else he had to say I have since forgotten. What I have always remembered is that question: 'How do you know?' As from that moment I realised that I must be prepared to defend every statement with fact and reason. But I was also allowed to believe, as were his other pupils, that my own opinion—resting on fact and reason—was as valid as that of the professor. This is the same intoxicating potion that Socrates would offer to his younger friends, with varying effects on them and an ultimately fatal result for himself. It is the first step in the scholar's progress, the throwing aside of the school textbook, the assumption of responsibility for one's own opinions. Here are two sayings which may serve to illustrate Welbourne's method of putting this lesson across:

> There is no better training in contemporary economics than the examination of the evidence heard by the Macmillan Commission; evidence given by the men who rule the big banks and by junior and unimportant economics lecturers at provincial universities. These men I do not feel to be my intellectual superiors; nor is their body of knowledge greater than mine. In fact, it is hardly greater than yours. If the sum total of knowledge is one bucket full, they possess a half while you possess a quarter bucket. But the difference is better realised thus: The total sum is like the Atlantic Ocean. They still have their half bucket and you still have half that—which means that the difference between you is comparatively small.

> The trouble with the professors is that they are all anxious to push their own theories and prevent their pupils from having their minds contaminated by the pestilent heresies of other professors. The advice of a college supervisor is much sounder. The chief thing to do is to read the original authorities thoroughly. A man who has read them three times is better off than the man who has only read them twice. And an intelligent man can

form his own opinion from them. What is more, his own opinion is as good as the professor's. Anyway, even if it weren't, it is better for him to have formed an opinion, even a wrong opinion, than not to have formed one. The man who has formed an opinion and then changed it, knowing *why* he has changed it, gets a First in the Tripos. It is better, on the whole, to work on your own and ignore the professors.

That was clearly what Welbourne himself had done, and it is sound advice for the student of initiative and intelligence. For another type of man it could be fatal, as Welbourne knew, varying his advice accordingly. In this connection it should be observed that Welbourne lectured, in my day, to a dwindling class, giving inspiration only to a last loyal handful. He always had a pile of notes to which he never referred, his lecture being probably about something else. He was the despair of the ardent note-taker and broke every rule in educational method. What he conveyed, to those who would listen, was the power of his personality and the quality of his mind. From him a few students, those happy few, learnt a certain down-to-earth attitude, a preference for the solid and unromantic fact. He had dismissed as rubbish most of what passes as classical history, the sentimental pictures of what later scholars believe to have happened in the world of their VIth Form imaginings. He saw the folly of basing a history on the merely literary sources which form the classicist's playground. He was as quick to see, however, where the medievalists and moderns go astray, biased as they may be by their own outlook in religion or politics. Concerned as he was with Law, I cannot believe that Welbourne was ever much more interested in constitutional history than he was in political theory. He was always, like Bluntschli in *Arms and the Man*, a lover of the prosaic. The following remembered sayings may serve to show how his mind always worked: 'Historically, the seller always comes before the buyer. It is the man with something to get rid of who comes hawking it round, not

the man who wants something who goes round trying to
get it.' 'Things like food and cooking and hot water bottles
are more important than mere railways.' 'Incense, like
livery and silver plate, was a weapon in the medieval war
against smells.' 'You either do or do not know how to
bleach with chlorine. If you don't know, you can't have an
Industrial Revolution. If you do, you can.' 'The trouble, or
part of the trouble with our agriculture now is that we
majestically pour all our manure into the North Sea, and
then go to South America to fetch guano.' 'The countryman
never cooked well because he had nothing but a wood-fire
to cook on.' 'The greatest crime in the Middle Ages was
cattle-stealing. For the man who stole your cattle and ate
them was striking at the root of civilization.' 'All the
Regency scandals happened in London. There was no help
for it until the railways came.' 'Monck had a sense of reality;
it was he who said, "It is no good giving the infantry
swords—they only use them for chopping wood." ' 'In 1870
people did not know that it was railways which had made
them prosperous. On the contrary, they *knew* it was
Methodist Chapels and flogging babies, self-denial and self-
help.' 'The motto of the 19th century should have been
"Honesty is the best policy—Now!" For Honesty is not the
best way to make money. But it *is* the best way to keep it.'
'The people of the Marshall school can throw bricks at me
for talking about imaginary reeves and villeins. Indeed,
they do, frequently. But I can throw bricks at them about
Marshall's pound of tea. He talked of the elasticity of tea
and of marginal utility in connection with tea. But he forgot
all the time that if you want more tea you don't buy more
tea. You send for more hot water.' In Welbourne's idea of
history elasticity goes out of the window, following constitutional progress and the Rights of Man. What remains?
Coal and guano, firewood and cattle dung, sidearms, chlorine
and pints of tea.

Welbourne's bluntness must have given offence to many
of his contemporaries. But a study of where his bricks fell

47

must reveal, incidentally, the targets he let alone. First of these was the College to which he had devoted his life. Linked to it in his mind were all groups of men whose lives are unpretentious, decent and hard. Linked with it again was, oddly enough, the Church of England where not too influenced by popery. Linked with it again was the life of the market town and countryside. Linked with it, finally, were all the young men who come up to Cambridge to study and play and argue, who spend their lives in scantily rewarded effort, who die too often on the battlefield, and whose sons apply for entry in their turn. Behind Welbourne's outspoken commentary there had always been an understanding, a sympathy and kindness, especially towards the young. He gained the affection as well as the admiration of his pupils and colleagues. No one of us could ever be uninfluenced by him. No one of us could ever forget him.

In trying to explain what I learnt from 'Teddy' Welbourne, I am speaking strictly for myself. Others will have learnt differently and some, I know, will have learnt much more. My own debt is at least tolerably clear. I came to Cambridge as an artist, with some inclination towards fiction and verse. I left Cambridge as a trained historian, with my field of interest already defined. I had learnt to dismiss both idealising and ideology, resting my story on the hard bedrock facts of geography, trade and war. 'One of our best possessions,' said Welbourne, 'was the world's supply of saltpetre. As a result we won all the wars for two hundred years.' This is the sort of hint any student could pursue. It led me to the verge of the history which has been most systematically ignored—the history of technology. Anyone can draw tactical diagrams, but there is more to the campaign than that. How did they mount their cannon? What was the quality of their propellant? Beginning with a background of naval history, going back to the days when I used to paint pictures of ships, I added to that a knowledge of economic history, derived from Welbourne, and an enthusiasm for the period of the Napoleonic Wars, taken from

Edward Welbourne

Professor Sir John Clapham. I thus ended, inevitably, as a maritime historian with a special interest in the period 1793–1815. I also ended with a habit of caustic assertion which other professors might deplore. 'I must confess I am surprised, and indeed a little alarmed,' wrote Welbourne in a letter to me, 'to find that your work allows you to hold so strongly views which I advanced . . . which are merely the result of thinking about my own general reading, and an apparently incurable personal habit of throwing all my own information into a somewhat unnecessarily defined shape.' He had some grounds, it may be, for alarm. But who, having known Welbourne, could wish to have been the pupil of anyone else?

From Welbourne, in the second place, I learnt to be intolerant of all that is deliberately inferior. There were and had been conflicts within the College, still more in the University, between the academically brilliant and those whose preference was for a mediocrity against which their own slight abilities could shine. Within the College the imperfectionists were routed and Welbourne's Mastership was itself the proof of their defeat. In the University School of History the conflict ended differently, and Welbourne foresaw how it would end:

'I have, I may almost confess to you,' he wrote to me in 1934, 'a personal desire to show that I shall be the father of as much history, through my pupils, as many of the historians in Cambridge whose natural membership of a mutual admiration society of "scholars" blinds them to greater truth. At the moment history is slipping into the hands of women, for they alone will work in seminars. They will kill it.' The murderers may prove to have been women of either sex, but they did their work with a certain finality. Cambridge of today contains scarcely a single historian of whom anyone has heard or needs to hear. It was a great subject in its day, but now it is dead.

As for Welbourne, he has been the father of more history, and more valuable history, than most of his contemporaries.

A Law Unto Themselves

In my own case, for what it is worth, I find in my notebooks a number of sayings from which later works were to derive. I shall content myself, however, with four:

The chief fact about modern States is that they have more and more people on their pay-roll.

If you have less than £25,000 a year you have to pay income-tax.

Everybody's idea of progress is simply this—more people like ourselves. The only exception is the man who has a revelation from God. And yet it often happens that the revelation is rather like oneself, too.

What gets work done well is not desire for good wages, but pride; pride and the love of playing with toys.

4

❧❧❧

GEOFFREY CALLENDER

There was a time when it was possible to know everything. The Oxford or Cambridge don who had graduated in classics and mathematics, taking holy orders and gaining some knowledge of law, could readily acquire three or four modern languages and could as easily read all that had been published in economics, science, geography and history.

> First come I. My name is Jowett.
> There's no knowledge, but I know it.
> I am Master of this College.
> What I don't know isn't knowledge.

The Victorians did not have to defend the study of the classics, for their men of learning were going to learn everything and might as reasonably begin with the classics as with anything else. They were not compelled to add much to the general fund of knowledge, although they occasionally did so, and the career devoted to learning was confined, in fact, to that. Unlike the Greek authors whose works they studied (authors who had little use for the classics) they were absorbed, above all, in books. As for history, it was mostly written outside the university by clergymen, landowners, administrators and bankers; by Maitland, Macaulay, by Freeman and Stubbs. When history was first introduced into the university syllabus it was with an air of apology. How make a serious subject of something which scholars had always taken in their stride? History crept in as an adjunct to law, as a minor aspect of theology. Its scope was defined by its first professors, its textbooks were

E 51

those they happened to approve. There was never a moment when historians asked themselves 'What are we trying to do?'

The historian's apology for his existence coloured the whole syllabus in my undergraduate years. It had often been asked whether history was not a soft option as compared with the classics. The answer to this was to deluge the freshman with Latin documents. Others then asked whether all this medievalism was relevant to the 19th century. It was pointed out, defensively, that statutes and leading cases are all so many stages in the development of the British constitution; each vitally important in itself and only to be understood in its historical context. This context had to involve the adjacent parts of Europe, however; partly to prove the similarities, partly to emphasise the contrasts. In modern history the story was one of Representative Government triumphant in Britain and belatedly copied on the Continent. The scientists asked at this point whether all this had any relevance to the future? But of course it had! There is, the historians replied, a science of politics—an application of history to current affairs, a synthesis of constitutional wisdom ready for the statesman's use. Political thought was thus established as a necessary part of the syllabus, the finish which crowned the whole. One other critic was the economist, who maintained that the Industrial Revolution was more important than the French Revolution. Economic History was the answer to that criticism, with Political Economy as an optional subject for study. There were thus, broadly speaking, two approaches to history; that of constitutional progress, ending with institutions and theories that could be exported to the colonies; and that of economic progress, ending with the industrial society which we had created mainly for ourselves.

This arbitrary deployment of effort did result in much useful work, but the undergraduate's first feeling was often one of frustration. He had previously acquired an interest in history as such, in the mere drama of past events; in exploration and discoveries, in personalities and battles, in cities and sickness, in music and sport. But he was told, in effect, that academic history was something different and apart, rigidly confined in terms of space, time and topic. It excluded the Ocean, all historical events taking place ashore. It excluded Asia, Africa and South America. It excluded, in fact, the vast majority of mankind and all civilisations which did not directly influence modern Europe. Having thus drawn a line round the facts of the world judged to be significant, the university historians ruled out some centuries as too remote and at least one century as too recent. They finally crossed off the history of science, technology, architecture, painting, medicine, warfare and sex. What had they left? They had Magna Carta to the Second Reform Bill, Stubbs to Trevelyan; Open Fields to Spinning Jennies, Cunningham to Clapham. All that can be said for this rigidity is that it made the subject examinable. As against that, the limits set were based on no obvious principle of selection. What is particularly momentous about the origin of Parliament? Why should it matter more than the origin of Association Football? Does it, actually, matter as much? Do textile factories influence mankind more than contraceptives or clocks? Must we always study the Enclosures and never look at horses or ships? Can we safely concentrate on the Risorgimento and forget about China? And why cannot the history student start, as he should, with the history of historians?

With so many questions unanswered, the academic historians have to face the onset of Social Science. In the eyes of the social scientist, history is no more than a subsidiary subject in his own department. Modern society is so different (he maintains) from anything previously known that its structure has to be analysed by the techniques of investigation, its history being only a minor aspect of its character. This argument is totally fallacious but the fallacy would be more obvious if the historians had ever considered what they are trying to do. Like the social scientists themselves, they are the victims of an historical process they have not troubled to analyse. The result is an over-concentration of effort in certain fields, an almost complete neglect of others. Naval History has been thus ignored at the universities, and so has Oriental History and the History of Science and Technology. And these were the areas of research to which I felt attracted, believing that their importance would eventually be recognised. In the meanwhile, as I knew, there was no university career open to the maritime historian. On the other hand there was the Royal Naval College at Greenwich, the home of the Society of Nautical Research, as also of the Navy Records Society. At Greenwich, I concluded, I should find a school of historians and a centre for research. Making my pilgrimage there in 1932, I thus made the acquaintance of Professor G. A. R. Callender, M.A., F.S.A., the Navy's official historian.

I have headed this chapter 'Geoffrey Callender' and that is the name which appears on his published books, but I never heard him addressed as 'Geoffrey' and imagine that he had been called by his initials 'G. A. R. C.' at Dartmouth; which gave rise to his nickname 'Garky', as used among the cadets. He was already middle-aged when I first met him, born in 1875 and his first book published in 1907. Moustached, spectacled, beak-nosed and bald, he was a rather Victorian figure and lived with his sisters in an extremely Victorian house. He was ageless in appearance, unaltered through the years, looking middle-aged (it is said) when he was fairly young and remaining middle-aged when fairly old. He was an inspired teacher but not a great historian, having done no real research. As against that, he had devoted himself to things maritime with an astonishing degree of concentration. He worked, when I first knew him, some eighteen hours a day, with weekends included and no holiday of any kind. I remember that he did once take a fortnight's rest at Budleigh Salterton, on medical advice. But all his correspondence had to follow him there and was dealt with in person, so that the main effect of the 'holiday' was to deprive him of secretarial assistance. He had an encyclopaedic knowledge of nautical archaeology but no liking for actual boats—at least, I never heard of his owning one or being seen afloat. His literary style was popular and breezy but somewhat dated, a survival from the period of Newbolt. The first book of his I read, *The Naval Side of British History*, was given to me by my brother in 1924 and made a great impression upon me at the time. Callender had, in the same way, influenced generations of young naval officers, giving them some feeling for history and indeed for literature. By the years immediately preceding World War II his *Sea Kings of Britain* had ceased to appeal, being out of place with the current mood. This may show the obsolescence of his style but does little to detract from his actual achievement, which was immense. In October 1932, when I first came to live at Greenwich, he was creating what was to become the National Maritime Museum; part of his effort going into the existing College, part into the future Museum. There was a hint of conflict between these two loyalties, heightened as it was by a proposal to put more work on the History and English Department, and embittered by disagreements with the President of the College, Vice-Admiral Barry Domville. The dispute was more vocal as between Domville and Brian Tunstall, who, with J. G. Bullocke, constituted the teaching staff; and Callender altered Canto VI of *Marmion* to suit the occasion:

> My sons command the vanward post
> With Brian Tunstall, stainless knight;
> Lord Dacre, with his horsemen light,
> Shall be in rear-ward of the fight. . . .

> Fitz-Eustace, to Lord Surrey hie;
> Tunstall lies dead upon the field.
> His life-blood stains the spotless shield;
> Edmund is down; my life is reft;
> The Admiral alone is left.

A Law Unto Themselves

It was Tunstall who in fact survived and Domville whose fascist views brought him into trouble. But Callender's tactics on this occasion were typical of him. He left the vanward post to others, and although he ruled the Society for Nautical Research for twenty-six years, I have heard it said that he was all but silent on its Council. In private, Callender had a gift for mimicry and wit, remarking for instance that 'When they make you wear a white waistcoat they ought to give you champagne. What is the point of a white waistcoat if there is no chance of spoiling it?' If amusing, he could also be waspish, leaving one to guess that the remarks he made about others would be matched, later, by the remarks he would make about oneself. He disliked most women, if not all, professed the strictest morality, and was jealous of all competition in his chosen field. His immediate colleagues, Tunstall and Bullocke, obviously detested him: his friends being more of his own generation. He was a regular communicant of a rather high Anglican church, a confirmed bachelor, a methodical worker, a prolific correspondent. After years of inhuman concentration he was no longer entirely sane.

My association with Callender began before I graduated and arose from the centenary of Lord Exmouth's death in 1833. Descendants of that distinguished admiral, feeling that the moment was right for a new biography, had approached Callender with an offer of all their unpublished family papers as raw material. He was their choice as biographer but Callender, who had other things to do, passed the assignment to me. Having saved a hundred pounds from my allowance at Cambridge, I had no need for immediate earnings so seized this opportunity to write a book. For a year I worked at Greenwich, therefore, in the Admiralty Library and at the Public Record Office, and the result was a work entitled *Edward Pellew, Viscount Exmouth, Admiral of the Red* published by Methuen in 1934 and well reviewed on the whole, in the London Press. By the time of its completion Callender offered me a post as his assistant in the embryo Museum, Michael Robinson being the other assistant, and both of us paid, initially, by the professor himself. I worked each day from 9.0 until 1.0, devoting the rest of the day to my own research, and was paid £1 a week for six mornings spent on the proofs of the Macpherson Collection Catalogue. Michael, I believe, worked all day for Callender and was rightly paid twice as much. As for me, I had entered the University of London as candidate for the Doctorate of Philosophy, and thus spent the next two years as pupil of Professor A. P. Newton, and as fifty per cent of the nascent Museum's assistant staff. After three years, all told, I could claim to have become a naval historian. I could also claim to know something of Callender's character and mission.

It was typical of 'Garky' that he would have nothing to do with the Greenwich Pageant of 1933. This should have been something close to his heart; a curtain-raiser, as it were, for the maritime glories to come. It was produced, however, by Arthur Bryant, and attempts to involve Callender as well—whether serious or half-hearted—must have failed at the outset. It became the accepted view in Callender's circle that the Pageant was designed primarily to gain Domville his knighthood. This was probably untrue —his appointment carrying that honour with it—and the Pageant was based more likely on somebody's realisation that Greenwich provides the perfect setting for a show of this kind. It might have become a regular event, like the Aldershot Tattoo, and a continual reminder that Greenwich exists. But Callender would have no part in it and would say nothing in its favour. We all chose to regard it as a mere interruption, an impediment to our normal work. And there was, admittedly, much to do. The basis of the Museum's intended display rested upon the Macpherson Collection, bought by Sir James Caird for this purpose in 1928, and the Admiralty's Collection in the College's Painted Hall. The essence of the plan was to shift all these and other exhibits into the Queen's House and adjacent buildings, vacated by the Royal Hospital School in 1932. The final step would then be to establish the new Museum by Act of Parliament, as was eventually done in 1934. As a corollary the Painted Hall would revert to its original purpose as a place in which to dine. All this sounds reasonably simple, but the work involved, the mere negotiation and argument, was enormous. Just one step among many—the one in which I happened to be involved—was the preparation of a catalogue which would convince the Prime Minister of the Museum's importance. Ramsay MacDonald was apt to fly hectically hither and thither and an advance copy of the catalogue had to be rushed to him before he started (I think for Scotland) so that he could tell Parliament about it on his return. It was I who delivered the bound copy to Sir James Caird, feeling for once like one upon whom a great responsibility had fallen. When the government wavered over the building costs, Caird solved the problem by paying for the structural work out of his own pocket. Considering all that had to be done, we may fairly conclude that Callender was to earn his knighthood before he got it.

From Callender I learnt both the possibilities and the limits of individual effort. My own hours of work were only a little fewer than his; four hours daily for him and twelve hours for research. Unlike him, however, I had to do this on £1 a week, doing my own cooking on a gas-ring and having therefore only one meal a day, at about 2.0 p.m. Except at the weekends I was at his office at 9.0 a.m. The day's work would usually end at some time between 1.0 and 3.0 a.m.—at the moment, in fact, when I could do no more. My original plan of research had been a logical development of my own first book. Edward Pellew was at one time Commander-in-Chief on the East Indies Station. Finding that no one had written the history of that Station during the French Wars, I had resolved to fill the gap; revealing simultaneously my interest in naval and oriental history, in the progress of technology and trade. Sir Herbert Richmond had written *The Navy in India, 1763–83*. It remained for

GEOFFREY CALLENDER

me to write the sequel from 1793 to 1815, prefacing the narrative with an account of the commerce which the warships were there to protect. The preface turned itself into another book and the thesis, when presented, ran to two volumes and 150,000 words; an infliction on the examiners which subsequent regulations were introduced to prevent.

Had Callender been a greater man than he was, I might well have spent my life as a maritime historian, proving that naval and economic history form different aspects of the same story. Clapham's pupils at Cambridge knew about trade but not about ships or colonies. A. P. Newton's pupils knew about colonies but not about war. Callender and his friends knew about ships but not about trade; nor indeed about historical research. I stood (as I liked to imagine) as the discoverer of a vast field of history which others had ignored or were unqualified to investigate. It would have taken a lifetime of effort to do what I could see needed doing. Could I, in effect, do for the Merchant Service what Callender had done, mainly, for the Royal Navy? Could I, for that matter, explain how the Navy fitted into the general pattern of history? These were reasonable questions to ask but the plan was destined to break down at two points. In the first place, there was no existing salaried position to which I could properly aspire. In the second place, I lacked Callender's singleness of purpose. I derived from my father and from Marylin Wailes a more generalised idea of success. I wanted more in material reward than a lifetime of scholarship was likely to offer. I took as my ideal not the dedicated effort of the medieval monk or modern scientist but the diffused accomplishment of the Elizabethan courtier. Callender was essentially a monk and well fitted for the intrigues of the chapter-house. I could work with something like his concentration, but the result could never have been its own reward. Scholarship was, for me, one aspect of a manly ideal, but only one. To achieve the right balance, one needed, surely, a wider range of accomplishment. One should have some skill in arms and poetry, some urge to travel, some gift for building, seamanship and art. According to the notions I had formed, Callender was not quite a scholar. Worse than that, he was not quite a man. All this may sound like the romanticism of youth as rationalised in middle age. But my own practice did accord, in some degree, with my theory. I was already, for one thing, an amateur soldier. I joined the 22nd London Regiment (The Queen's) in 1934, being gazetted Lieutenant. I had learnt something of swordsmanship and Judo while at College. I was still physically active, my Pellew biography involving a cycle ride to the places with which he was connected; a ride, as it happened, from York to Dover, from Dover to Penzance, from Penzance up the West of England into Lancashire and so home across the Pennines. I had studied in Paris and followed the career of St Joan from Chinon to Orleans and from there to Rouen. I had studied, on the ground, the siege of La Rochelle. As an oarsman I had helped take a boat as far up the Yorkshire Swale as the craft could be made to go. I had walked in the Pyrenees and come near to drowning in the Loire. Callender could never have been my ideal as a personality. In his field of learning my ideal was rather Sir Herbert Richmond, the Admiral turned historian; the Master, eventually, of Downing College. But his career, as I was eventually to learn, had fallen short of its expected goal; mainly, I believe, because his interests were divided between action and letters. On a far lower level of achievement I stood in danger, perhaps, of making the same mistake. For the moment, however, my original gamble after graduation would seem to have succeeded. Instead of seeking a position as schoolmaster in 1932 I had sought my fortunes in London. My efforts were rewarded in 1935. In May of that year I commanded a company of infantry at the Jubilee of King George V. In June I learnt of my election into a Research Fellowship at my own College. In October I learnt that the University of London had awarded me a Doctorate of Philosophy. In December I learnt that I had been awarded the Julian

Corbett Prize. In the academic sense, I had more or less arrived. My life as a penniless student had come to an end and its completion was marked by a funeral; that of the old King himself. With his passing a phase of British history came to its end.

The 22nd London Regiment were among the troops ordered to line the route of the Funeral Procession. When it was all over, on January the 29th, 1936, I wrote my mother an account of the day's duty in a letter which has survived and which reads as follows:

Owing to my orders not reaching me, my first intimation that I should be on duty came in the form of a telegram on Friday evening. As this came too late for me to attend a rehearsal that night, I was in doubt as to whether they would need my services. However, I got a trunk-call through, at the fourth attempt, on Monday afternoon. The reply was 'Come at once'. I got into uniform and reached H.Q. that evening. After I had learnt the ritual, I went to bed there at midnight, having borrowed some blankets and a camp-bed. I was up at 4.0 and spent the next hour and a half cleaning my kit, washing and shaving. The other officers began to arrive at 5.30 and we had breakfast a little before 6.0. Half-an-hour later we embarked in several hired buses, with about two hundred men. It was still dark. Going by a rather circuitous route around the vicinity of Westminster, we were near Marble Arch by daybreak, soon after 7.0. It poured with rain on the way but it had ceased before we arrived. We fell in just inside Hyde Park and marched up Edgware Road. We halted three or four hundred yards along it, having to push through a dense crowd to get there. People had been on the curb since the night before, and the centre of the road was filled with people, all looking for places from which to see the procession. It seemed as if both troops and police had come on the scene too late. We quickly extended on both sides of the road, other units doing the same until the cordons were complete. The people in the middle wandered up and down, some being told to go one

61

way, some the other. Most of them merely wanted to escape. In the end, the police chivvied them northwards, but I don't know where they went to. By now the crowd on either side was too closely packed to get through, and it would have caused a riot to allow stray people to stand in front of the earlier arrivals. Anyway, these thousands dwindled away somehow. Among them were people who had paid for seats in shops but could not get there. Meanwhile, people kept pouring up the side-streets and the press got worse and worse. In the distance, at Marble Arch, we could see that the crowd had broken through the police and troops. Presently, in our own area, the densely packed mob swayed forward and pushed into the road. Our colours were nearly engulfed, but were rescued in time. As our line of troops and police began to give way, we hurled in more men and tried to drive the crowd back. With rifles pushed into them and banged on their toes, the people in front gave way a little. But they could not move far because of the mass behind. We threw in more men and pushed like a 'rugger' scrum. But the route was still half-blocked at the point where a side road came in from the east. More police arrived and then some mounted police tried to drive them in. It was no good. At the Marble Arch end of the road, where the block was worse, they were using cavalry, but with precious little result. It can hardly be wondered at that, with the pressure from behind, and our attacks from the front, the press became too much for people. They fainted or were injured and the St John's Ambulance men began to carry them off by dozens, women mostly and a few old men and children. According to today's papers there were ten thousand casualties in all, and five hundred at our point near Marble Arch. There were hundreds collapsing behind our cordon and being dragged out. They got them away by a narrow lane through the crowd on the west side, some on stretchers and some carried. The St John's Ambulance men were numerous and efficient, but their rescues (some women were handed over the heads of the crowd, when the ambulance men could not get to them) did not seem to lessen the mob. And we still had to drive people in when the pressure became too great. We had sheathed our swords—the officers, I mean—so as not to injure people. This went on for over two hours and things were no better when the first gun was fired to show that the procession had started. A police car came up with a megaphone on the roof, through which an officer appealed (in vain) to the crowd's better feelings. Assistant-Commissioners rode up in cocked hats, but the police failed in all their efforts, clearly not knowing what to do. We realised that half our men were too much embroiled in the fray to reverse or present arms when the procession came. The minute guns fired in Hyde Park told us that it was getting near, as it was due to do. No remedy, however, was found; and the procession had to squeeze through as best it could. The head of it appeared at the end of the road. We drew swords again and reversed arms. Apart from a few minutes at the 'present' when the gun-carriage passed, followed by the Royal Family, we had to rest on our arms reversed for exactly fifty-five minutes—standing perfectly still that is, with head down and our eyes on the ground. I could see a little by squinting up and sideways, and of course I saw the King as we presented arms. Also I was privileged to move twice during the time the procession passed; once was when someone fainted just behind me and I had to shift to allow the ambulance men to remove the body; and once was when, owing to the narrowness of the way, an Air Force officer walked into me. He was looking back over his shoulder, marshalling the procession, and not watching where he was going. The massed pipes were rather wonderful—I hope you were listening in. There was no other sound but the bands, the minute guns, and (for a few minutes) the swish of the rain as it came pelting down on the Kings and the Captains. The crowd stood still enough until the tail-end of the procession came. By that time my feet were numb and I was glad to move again.

On looking round, I saw that the men had all been pushed forward at some time, and were still leaning back in places to hold the crowd. I noticed that my sword was covered with spots of rust. We closed quickly round our colours and the crowd surged all round us so that we could scarcely keep our ranks. It was no good waiting for the street to clear. We moved off in file and cut our way out of it as we could, the leading officer driving people out of the way with his sword. With another officer I did the same, one of us on each side of the colours, to protect them. And so we won a way through, presently finding ourselves back in the park. . . .

One thing I remember from that occasion but failed to comment upon, was the white-faced appearance of Edward VIII, who looked near death himself; aware already perhaps of how it might all end. It was a bad moment to weaken the monarchy by the folly he had set in train. How threatening the international situation was I was soon to realise. Going abroad that summer with my brother, who was to hold the temporary post as Chaplain of the Embassy Church in Rome, I saw the place of the Nazi 'Martyrs' in Munich and was present in Salzburg for the second anniversary of the assassination of Dollfuss. At Bozen or Bolzano I saw a parade of Fascist young men, bound for the Olympic Games at Berlin; not as competitors, I learnt, which was possibly just as well, for they appeared to be drunk. In Rome I saw the Spanish Embassy divided against itself into two warring factions. At Padua every inch of wall space had been stencilled with slogans such as '*Duce a noi*', '*Viva il Duce*' and '*Viva Guerra*' and announcements that Italy stood against the world. In Venice I found a picture of Mussolini pasted upon every column in the Piazza S. Marco, and it was there that I saw Goebbels, escorted by obsequious Fascists and applauded by a small crowd. Altogether, I glimpsed that year a most unsettled Europe, being only slightly consoled by an amateur German fortune-teller who told me that I was romantic, musical, sometimes hesitating and shy, and foretold for me a successful career, a long life with two great changes and the begetting of at least one child. It seemed to me that one great change I had already experienced and that Adolf Hitler was ready to provide the second.

5

EVAN JOHN

It was in the course of rehearsal for some London show that my mother's friend, Dorothy Holmes-Gore, first met Evan John Simpson. He was tall, slim, spectacled, with a small and slightly puckered face, a high forehead and a receding shock of untidy fairish hair. Full of enthusiasm and bubbling with ideas, he had the most beautiful hand-writing I have ever seen, Eric Gill's alone excepted. Born in 1901 and educated at Winchester and Oxford, he listed his hobbies as fencing and carpentry and omitted to mention his skill as a painter. But all these activities related directly to his career on the stage. This could have begun at Oxford where he won a University Scholarship with a thesis on Shakespeare's life as an actor. He must have been stage-manager when they met, for Dorothy noticed first of all that he was always to be seen on a ladder with a hammer or paint-brush, nails in his pocket and a screw-driver between his teeth. They were married in 1930 and that is how I came to know Evan John. He was partly of Scottish origin, his father a Home Office official who had to take the blame for some departmental error, retiring thus prematurely and refusing the knighthood which was to have been his consolation prize. He was perhaps an impulsive man, having married a half-Greek lady as the result of a few days' acquaintance at the revived Olympic Games of 1896. He had no reason to repent at leisure what had been done in haste. The marriage was a happy one and lasted for fifty years. Although proud of his family, Evan John described his surname as just right for a cricketer but unsuitable for the stage or for authorship. He was a good character actor but was more intent on making himself a name as producer and dramatist. By the time I came to work at Greenwich, writing my first book, he was already stage-managing at the Westminster Theatre under Amner Hall. He had earlier been with Amner Hall for a year at the Festival Theatre, Cambridge, working in conjunction with Tyrone Guthrie. The Westminster was an intimate theatre, as now, and boldly experimental; so much so that it was Evan John—not the more experienced Tyrone Guthrie—who was given the chance to produce James Bridie's *Tobias and the Angel*. He did this extremely well but saw his own future as a dramatist. His play *The Dark Path* had been performed at the Savoy Theatre in 1928, being followed by *Two Kingdoms* in 1934, which was moved to the Westminster. It is a romantic play in verse about 16th-century Japan, dealing with the impact of Christianity on the traditional society of that land. A sincere Christian himself, Evan John had a lively interest in things oriental, as indeed in what Shakespeare called 'the World's Debate'. I found *Two Kingdoms* fascinating as an art form, as a discussion of ideas and as a clue to Evan John's philosophy.

In *Two Kingdoms* (Arthur Barker, London, 1935) Evan John shows his poetic gift and also his mastery of the rhymed couplet as used so effectively by Dryden. Here is a sample:

KURAMA: God is the wind, and God the thunderstorm:
        God is the scarlet of the evening sky.
        The lonely bird that drifts in silence by:
        God is man's kindly worth and woman's grace,
        The sweet, shy glances on my mistress' face:
        God is the wit that barbs your restless tongue.
KATO: The priests said 'twas the Devil.
KURAMA: They were wrong.

To a real sense of poetry there is joined here the neat, concise and skilful play of ideas and words and wit.

F

A Law Unto Themselves

Here fight two kingdoms, Europe and Japan.
Here fight two kingdoms for the soul of Man.
. . . .
They preach, he prays, time passes, and I wait.

It is the strictness of the metre which gains the effect but Evan John had also something of importance to say. It was with him I first discussed the basic conflict between East and West. 'The kings of the East were ever travellers', he makes one character say. 'We have wandered from Oxus to the Indies, from Babylon to the magic rampart that guards China from our spears. Our cities are not as the cities of the West; they are but halting places for our caravans. . . .' He had thought deeply about this sort of contrast but without any attempt to be impartial. Like G. K. Chesterton, his idol and mine, he knew which side he was on. In temperament he was a Crusader, needing a great cause into which he could throw himself. In the right circumstances he could display a tireless energy, a wide knowledge of life and history, a keen traveller's sense of locality, a forceful eloquence, a lively wit (more than humour) and an intense concentration on the matter in hand. He was a man who could accomplish much, whose mind ranged from the greatest issues to the detailed use of chisel and saw. All that he lacked, at first, was the actual Crusade. Its place, in his thinking, was taken by the Civil War.

For Evan John far more than for most people the Cavalier Cause was still alive. He once founded a Cavalier Club, of which I was a member, and discussions were held among the members as to how Charles I should have been better advised. The Cavaliers of history were more Anglican, perhaps, than Monarchist; but for Evan John the idea of Kingship was sacred in itself. The proof of this lies in the very titles of his published works: *King-at-Arms*, 1932; *King Charles I* (biography), 1933; *Two Kingdoms*, 1935; *The King's March*, 1937; and *King's Masque*, 1941. The case for monarchy had been stated by G. Bernard Shaw in *The Apple*

Evan John

Cart (1929) but Evan John really believed in it and was ready to explain why. While Alphonso XIII was being tried, in his absence, at Madrid in 1931, Evan John wrote a play based on that theme. His King Charles IV, of Great Britain, is also to be tried *in absentia* (in A.D. 2008) but prefers to appear in person. Whether his case for the defence is proved may be thought doubtful but he deals faithfully at least with the House of Commons and the Party System:

> CHARLES: I mean that shameless parody which you cover with the sacred name of democracy which might have been devised for throwing to the top those who are least fitted to govern. Pardon me, gentlemen, if I grow personal: you force it upon me. You may once have been ordinary men, suitable representatives of my people— until you decided to become politicians. On that day you were caught up into an atmosphere of words and phrases that mean nothing to the ordinary man and woman. You climb above your fellows, you earn money by a skilful manipulation of meaningless things, by affecting publicly to believe what in private you know to be meaningless. You make your compromise—a little more or a little less —with that corruption which flourishes upon all un- reality. Then, when you have dazed your voters with your speeches, your newspaper articles and your election- eering, you choose out another man from the same clique as yourself, equally corrupt, equally unfitted to govern. You call yourself by one label, your colleague, misnamed opponent, by another, and you say—'Choose between us.' . . . And you dare to tell us that the winner of this undignified game speaks with the divinely inspired voice of my People?

> (*King-at-Arms*. Arthur Barker, London, 1935, p. 80)

The play ends with a monarchist revolution and the last line 'It's time England was governed.' So indeed it was but Evan John was fighting for a hopeless cause and one which King Edward VIII killed outright. Nor could this Cavalier playwright bring much ammunition to the field of battle. He knew little of politics and less of administration, lacking even G. B. Shaw's experience on a Borough Council. One thing he perceived, however, was that the British Empire could not last for ever. In practice, it did not even last for long.

Evan John's first and only contact with monarchy came in the very last years of his life, in 1953. News of the earthquake in the Ionian Islands reached him on August the 13th and he flew quixotically to the rescue, determined to do what he could for the homeless. It was little in fact he could do and the Royal Navy was ahead of him. He was witness, nevertheless, to what was done and asked rhetorically 'whether the world has ever seen such a combination of organisation and courtesy, hard-headedness and sympathy, courage, needful ceremony and unwearying common sense as our nation has perfected during its chequered centuries of admiralty'. He pushed on nevertheless with his own crazy mission and presently found himself in conversation at Phrikes with a Greek officer whose jeep stopped beside him. Asked what he was doing, Evan John said that he was there as representative of the British Friendship to Greece Society, the objects of which he went on to explain. He ended by asking the Greek officer for his name, and was told, with a laugh, 'But I'm the King of Greece.' Having made his apologies, Evan John ended with the words, 'But I expect your Majesty has rather enjoyed all this.' 'To which the King replied, 'I have!' Deeply moved by this encounter—as was Dr Johnson by his meeting with George III —Evan John summarised his reaction in *Time after Earthquake* which proved to be almost his last published work.

. . . I cannot understand how anyone, whether of romantic, prosaically modern, or even revolutionary temperament, can fail to be moved by contact with persons round whom hover the hopes and fears, the greeds and aspirations of many millions of poor and humble folk. And the experience must surely be a little more memor-

Evan John

able when such brief contact suggests that they are worthy representatives of that tremendous mass of human feeling which they have been born to symbolize, and can sometimes help to direct.

(Heinemann, London, 1954)

Some might think this an unexpectedly sensible conclusion to have been reached by one gifted, by his own account, with an unusual deficiency in common sense.

Talented as Evan John obviously was, he had three drawbacks as a colleague or ally. In the first place, he could be quarrelsome. It is true that the fit of anger passed and that he was quick to apologise or forgive; but the damage had sometimes been done, especially among theatre folk less generous than he. I fancy that his stage career may have been interrupted and spoilt by wrathful incidents which made him seem more difficult than he was. No other of my acquaintance has actually challenged a brother officer to a duel, defying *King's Regulations* and every accepted convention of the day. In the second place, his taste was for the colourful and dramatic. His talent could never have been enlisted in any drab cause to do with housing or the welfare of the poor. Like many another actor, he could be suspected, often perhaps wrongly, of preferring romance to reality. In the third place, he could become more excited than would have been possible for someone whose mental balance was perfect. These blemishes apart, Evan John was ordinarily among the most stimulating of companions; the leader in any conversation, the centre of any group, the leading spirit in any enterprise, and Dorothy, his wife, was quite as intelligent and more amusing; adding the common sense which he occasionally seemed to lack.

In 1938 Evan John published *Crippled Splendour*, a fictional biography of James I of Scotland 'Prisoner, Poet, Musician, Soldier, Law-Giver and King'—and author, incidentally, of the *King's Quair*. This was a Book Society

Choice and a bestseller, its success marking the end of his career as dramatist and actor. As the stage would know him no more, he wisely retired to a property he bought at Wyfold, near Reading.

> I was quitting London [he wrote] because (after writing in my spare time for some twenty years and making during all that period rather less than fifty pounds) I had suddenly gained much more money than was good for me from the proceeds of one historical novel—a species of literature I had hitherto tended to despise. I used it to buy myself an ugly but delightfully situated farmhouse, among Chiltern beechwoods.
>
> (*Time in the East.* Heinemann, London, 1946, p. 4)

The historical novel is a difficult type of literature, the author's task being to strike some sort of balance between historic fact and acceptable fiction. The great historical novels in the English language (perhaps in any language) are thus relatively few. After the days of Scott and Thackeray, the classics range from *The Cloister and the Hearth* by Charles Reade, to *Richard Yea-and-Nay* by Maurice Hewlett—with R. L. Stevenson's *Black Arrow* in about the same class. But Reade and Hewlett, having each produced a masterpiece, were respectively unwilling and unable to do it again. Evan John was not quite in their class. He had, nevertheless, some of C. S. Forester's gift for conveying technical information. He was an expert, for example, in fencing with sword and dagger as well as foil. A pupil of Gravé, he knew that a stage duel, properly rehearsed, should illustrate the plot and characters better than any spoken line. But, apart from that, he could make others share his enthusiasm. As his opponent on one occasion, I can remember the initial difficulties encountered by one trained, as I had been, with foil and sabre; difficulties which many actors fail eternally to overcome. In *Crippled Splendour* the swords and lances are real, as they are, for that matter, in Robert Graves' *Belisarius.* The women, unfortunately, are not.

Evan John

And this is where Evan John failed equally as a dramatist. He knew love and marriage and fatherhood but his fictional women never quite came to life, save possibly in *Ladies Beware*. As serious, perhaps, was his inexperience in matters of administration, politics, finance and war. Like G. K. Chesterton he was quick to see what was wrong but he was no better than G. K. C. in suggesting how it should be put right. Some practical experience he was about, however, to have. While war was still merely imminent he 'took the obvious step of enlisting as a gunner in the local battery of Territorial Artillery'. This step was less obvious to some other intellectuals of his generation.

It was Evan John's belief that World War II became inevitable after the Italian bombardment of Corfu in 1923. That incident proved the possibility of getting away with murder. It proved the futility of the League of Nations. It proved finally that Britain was virtually leaderless, with no one ready to act as Palmerston would have advised. To Evan John, as to many of us, the British declaration of war in 1939 came as something of a relief. We were prepared at last to do what we might have done—so easily and economically—in 1923. In the resulting conflict Evan John had found his Crusade and one more melodramatic than he could have imagined. It took him first into the bloodless raid on the Lofoten Islands, where in six minutes he learnt more (he said) of discipline than he could have learnt in six years of peacetime training. 'War is not a reasonable business; reasoning about it, even reasoning about the training for it, is always in danger of becoming argument about it. And he who argues or lets others argue is Lost.' With this important lesson learnt, he went on to an O.C.T.U. and was commissioned in the Intelligence Corps before being posted to G.H.Q. Middle East. His chief delight had always been in travel and he was now entitled to do this, within limits, at the public expense. Taking full advantage of his opportunities, he covered much of the terrain of the Crusades and did so, often enough, on horseback. The immediate result of

73

A Law Unto Themselves

his many odd adventures in Palestine, Syria and Lebanon was *Time in the East, an Entertainment,* published in 1946. This is as near as he came to writing his autobiography and the book tells us more indeed about the author than it does about the war. He claimed at the time that this compilation 'consumed much time which would otherwise have been devoted to clogging the Wheels of War with more and more of that paper which at times threatens to bring them to a standstill'. The claim was justified but the book had only a very moderate success; nor, for security reasons, did it even contain all the fruits of his experience. He was concerned with counter-espionage and I recall his telling me that most spies work for both sides and are known to do so, but that their consuming motive is not greed so much as vanity. They like to feel that they are at the heart of affairs and swaying the destinies of mankind. Little of the information they have to peddle is in fact of any value, but no country at war can afford to despise any card in the pack. For what it is worth, the British are usually more astute at this game than their allies or opponents. But Evan John was saddened to discover that security techniques always include torture and that no society could survive without its occasional use. He also discovered that, while there may be no heroes in real life there are certainly villains. 'I began to understand,' he wrote, 'what I had once thought I should never understand—how a rogue's escape from his penalty may be considered as grave a miscarriage of justice as an innocent man's condemnation,' and how the results may be infinitely worse. He ended by seeing the necessity for the firing squad and the gallows, concluding, with Shakespeare, that 'Mercy but murders, pardoning those that kill'—or those who, worse, betray.

Involved as he was in the war and resolute in playing the game for his side, Evan John had no illusions about the bureaucracy of which he temporarily formed a part. A brief pre-war period as Air Raid Warden had left him appalled by the ineptitude of the official advice he was sup-

EVAN JOHN

posed to pass on; 'The enemy will use a heavy gas, lethal at ground level,' which tended to suggest that the best place was the attic. Sage counsel of this sort was relatively harmless, for none but a born fool would have heeded it for a moment, but other nonsense could be traced to more apparently reliable sources. Some trace of bitterness on this score crept into Evan John's writing, as in his verses dated from the Hotel de Luxe at Jerusalem:

> Young Pontius Pilate, with gleaming Sam Browne,
> Sipping pink gin as he passes the buck,
> 'I've washed my hands of it. Turned the job down.
> 'Tisn't my pigeon if things come unstuck.'

And quite apart from what people did or avoided doing, there was something appalling in their mere numbers. It was said in those days that an attack by Rommel on Cairo, compelling G.H.Q. personnel to turn out in their own defence, would have found the Germans outnumbered for the first time. As for the files to which anyone might wish to refer, they were gradually 'ranked and multiplied and catalogued out of sight.' Observing this trend, as we all did in those days, Evan John perceived the further danger of persisting in peacetime with the extravagances which are one result of war.

... You have only to plant a subaltern in some suitably requisitioned building, and give him, perhaps, one batman-clerk-driver. You need not water or manure, and he will resist all efforts to prune. Come back in eighteen months and you will find that he has blossomed out into a Major, with two Captains to assist him and two budding Lieutenants as 'stooges'. There will be a healthily-multiplying rose-bed of typists, and a patch of rubbish heap, where native elements, messengers and coffee-makers will have got their roots well dug in. At first sight, the whole organisation will appear to be doing exactly the same work that the subaltern had done before, unaided. Actually it has the added burden of organizing its own

pay and allowances, preventing overlapping of labour,
assuring the welfare of its O.R.'s and petitioning for
further increase of establishment or the requisition of
larger premises.

If there is exaggeration in this picture, there is a large
kernel of truth. Supposing the present 'Money doesn't
matter' attitude survives the Peace Treaty, it augurs ill
for our post-war life. Even if we can afford to go on
throwing away Cash by handfuls, I doubt if we can go on
throwing away Time. And I am sure we cannot afford to
throw away any more Liberty. Bureaucracy is a habit,
easily growing into a vice, and the habit of interfering
with other people's lives is an easy one to acquire. Put
any man into office, and he may be an addict within
six months. And he may never be able to shake the
habit off.

(Time in the East. Heinemann, 1946, p. 190)

The war taught Evan John a great deal about administration. Without becoming a bureaucrat himself he came to
know what bureaucracy is. More than that, he gained some
idea of tactical principles as applied to the Middle East. As
an historical novelist he gained enormously from this contact with actual events. If Edward Gibbon owed something
to his service in the Militia, Evan John was to owe still
more to his service in the Army. How much he owed became apparent after the war when he had returned to Neal's
Farm, to authorship and carpentry. *Ride Home Tomorrow*
was his last important book and it marked a great advance
on all that he had previously written. It seemed to fore-
shadow a literary career of growing importance.

The action of this story began in Norway but takes place
otherwise in the medieval Kingdom of Jerusalem. Dealing
with a country which he knew well, with a sort of warfare of
which he had some actual experience, with a horsemanship
and swordsmanship he had carefully studied, Evan John
wrote now with a new realism. He had perceived, first of
all, that war is not the continuous conflict of the cinema but

Evan John

a way of life in which brooding and distant menace forms the background to many activities which are otherwise unremarkable, frivolous or dull. *Time in the East* represents, as it were, a preliminary study of warfare in the setting of the Crusades. It reveals, among other things, the author's recently acquired respect for the oriental mind. *Ride Home Tomorrow* represents the next stage in the author's development; a concentration of his experience and skill upon a task for which he was almost uniquely qualified. To me, this last historical novel is his best. The scenes and characters are remarkable, the atmosphere cleverly indicated and the prose often masterly. Where he failed once more, was with the heroine, who never quite comes to life. We learn indeed of the hero's feelings for her, but can only guess at her own attitude to him or to anyone else. What chiefly remains of the book in subsequent recollection is the impatience felt by the veteran for the novice, the detailed knowledge of the old campaigners which they can hardly bother to share. Those deeply involved in a war evolve a language of their own and a set of conventional attitudes towards the enemy and the country, towards civilians and towards each other. All this Evan John had experienced, from both points of view, and this is what he was most successful in describing. But his battles are real enough and the more so for being relatively infrequent. He used to build up skilfully towards his crisis, and his picture of disaster at the Horns of Hattin is a masterpiece in its way. He cannot be compared, of course, with Maurice Hewlett; but then, who can? At his own level, he wrote very well indeed. One of his themes, in conversation, was the book that Hilaire Belloc should have written, a Military Geography of Europe. In the same way, the novel which Evan John should have written would have centred upon the Great Siege of Malta. Dealing with the celibate Knights of St John he would have had no need of a heroine, and in Jean Parisot de la Valette he would have had his principal character ready made. In point of fact, however, his last writings ranged from *The*

Network, a novel based upon the Canadian Spy Trials, to *Atlantic Impact*, the story of how nearly Britain and U.S.A. went to war with each other in 1861. He argued, incidentally, that the decline of the British Empire began with the cession of the Ionian Islands in 1862; giving additional importance to the same period. All this work was competently done, but he had no real interest—as I think—in the post-war world. The struggle with Communism might be regarded as a Crusade but hardly of the sort he could best appreciate. Like Sir Walter Scott he had a love of war in its more picturesque form. He had to have horses and armour,

HENRY THE FIFTH During the period of this play there was no change in the royal arms (fig. 48 p. 31.) Henry used as badges A Fire Beacon: A white Swan gorged and chained (fig. rather than the tame swimmer of Australia and Messrs Malie Todd): and An Antelope (hained (see fig. 69.). It is a little difficult to believe that tradition is right in ascribing to his son, Henry VI., the adoption of Dieu et mon Droit as the royal motto. The words seem to express so exactly Henry V's peculiar blend of piety and aggressiveness.

FROM AN ILLUMINATED M.S. BY EVAN JOHN.

heraldry and battlements, crossbows and helmets, lances and swords.

Evan John's growing maturity as a novelist was not paralleled by any stabilising of his personality. He was appointed after the war to a post in the British Council, not as a propagandist of British culture but as an executive on the personnel side. His paper qualifications might have seemed appropriate but the offer was crazy, and his acceptance crazier still. It ended, inevitably, in his abrupt dismissal for reasons unstated but imaginable. He returned to authorship and travel, working with spasms of energy which alternated with fits of depression. These periods of blackness he had evidently experienced for years. He describes them in *Time in the East* with an almost clinical listing of the symptoms:

> All life rearranged itself into a cruel pattern of torment. Material trifles, like telephones or washing-lists, became instruments of tragedy or insurmountable barriers to action. My fellow men and women—and myself with them—turned into utterly self-centred beasts of prey, cloaking behind sickening masks of politeness, sentimentality and self-deception, our lust and callousness, our greed and our ultimate despair. No kind of faith, hope or charity had, or could have, any meaning in this world or another. I lay awake at night or got up to march endlessly round empty streets. . . . There seemed to be no refuge but in suicide, and for that I lacked the enterprise. I can remember standing on pavement edges in London streets and feeling a muscular reaction tending to throw me under the wheels of passing traffic. . . . Not merely the power to fight, but the reason for fighting, the innermost springs of all courage and resolution, seemed to be cut away from within me, and in their place was an unintelligible blank.
>
> (Heinemann, 1946, p. 103)

These periods of depression would last three weeks or more, straining his power of survival to the utmost. Then, inevitably, the crisis came, with misery more intense than he could bear. We corresponded very occasionally and in December 1953 I had sent him a bottle of wine as a gift. He was, I believe, in the act of writing to thank me when the burden of life became too great. He took his own life that day and so put an end to his torment. In *King-at-Arms* he made his King Charles IV speak as follows:

> ... We're mere children, you know; we can't expect to see very far. We can only play the game on what seems to be the right side; and it isn't long before we have to pack up our toys and go to sleep. ... I shan't be sorry when it's bedtime.
>
> (Arthur Barker, London, 1935, p. 80)

The last letter I had from Evan John, or the last that I have kept, is dated on January the 11th, 1950. Here I have to go to the post-war period, far out of autobiographical sequence, so as to complete the story. By that period my first marriage had ended in disaster. Lacking Evan John's periods of depression—for the same reason that I lacked his poetic vision—I thought less of suicide than of leaving the country. His letter was written fairly shortly before I did so.

> I am indeed sorry to hear of you quitting England, and feeling you may never want to come back. Feelings change. They can even change (My God they can!) about marriage—another matter on which I am a fanatical Tory, not blaming anyone for a divorce, but frenziedly blaming a social system and atmosphere which makes divorce seem any way out of anything. I won't foolishly presume to offer advice or comment upon any individual case. I wait and watch.
> I'll only say one thing. Whatever reasons people give for breaking up their marriages, one can always be sure of one thing—that they are the wrong reasons. The right ones, in my experience, always lie far too deep to be articulate or even conscious. ...

Evan John

All that is true enough and what Evan John had to say was both helpful and wise. But the social reticence in which he believed was a handicap to him as a novelist. His own emotional life remained his own affair, shared only with one other, and no hint of it appeared in his published work. Books thus lacking a dimension could succeed only up to a certain point. Apart from that, moreover, he stood aside, and deliberately, from the age in which he lived. His Toryism was too Tory for the Conservatives, his loyalty too loyal for the King. In the post-war world, the farce that followed melodrama, there was no part that he could play.

We are not to know how his literary gifts might have developed during the later years that should have been his. He might have mellowed and found that sense of proportion which he lacked at the outset. He might have learnt how to bring his heroines to life. As against that, his last and posthumous novel, *The Darkness*, shows no sign of it. In that he deals with the period after the crucifixion, giving an imaginatively detailed description of events we know only in barest outline. The book uses again the background of a country known to him. It reveals no loss of energy or skill and yet falls short, in some ways, of *Ride Home Tomorrow*. The theme was one, to him, of paramount importance, and his awareness of this makes him too careful to avoid heresy. The book was well reviewed, nevertheless, and deservedly so for the skill with which he made the story real and vivid. Like his other books it well illustrates the difference between wit and humour. Of wit he had plenty but of humour all too little, a contrast well illustrated in his defence of A. A. Milne, whose more serious plays upset the critics:

> They dubbed you jester, and though we were glad you
> Showed deeper thoughts, for which your jests were blinds,
> The critics disagreed. For what right had you
> To ask those gentlemen to change their minds?

This is neatly done, in the manner of Dryden or Swift, but shows too little sense of A. A. Milne's special quality. For while A. A. M. could be serious on occasion, and even momentarily bitter, his humour was seldom used to cloak any specially solemn message. He laughed mostly for sheer enjoyment of all that is absurd. He loved people and loved them the more for being funny.

Humour springs directly from the sense of proportion. Without a clear idea of the proper relationships between things and people we can have no sharp perception of the incongruous. For humour we need, above all, an ordered world; the England, for example, which A. A. Milne knew in his younger days. Evan John glimpsed that for a short period—and I for a still shorter time, a matter of months—but he lacked, in any case, the mental stability upon which real humour depends. And while I learnt a great deal from him, more especially from his sense of theatre and feeling for geographical background (two aspects of the same thing), I also had to regard him as a warning of mistakes to avoid, and chiefly the error of taking too many things too seriously. When that has been said, however, the fact remains that Evan John could write. Let me quote him again, allowing the reader to judge for himself:

There was coolness and freshness on that upper road, though the icy blasts that sweep Jerusalem in winter were now tempered into pleasant breezes, the Spring rains abating and the snows of a hard Christmas almost forgotten. Jerusalem, unlike Acre, is no town for sluggards: its air is the most invigorating I have ever breathed, its colour bright and clear and exciting. Men and women are tempted to do too much rather than too little in that stone-built city among the hills, to talk too much, quarrel too often, love too passionately and hate too bitterly. Here God died, and here Satan still has power to arm his lusting servants to killing, and to the sins which lead more deviously to bloodshed. Yet it remains for me, who have seen many cities, the most beautiful on earth.

(*Ride Home Tomorrow*. Heinemann, London, 1950, p. 160)

Evan John

I dream sometimes of finding a place where there is no need of government, of the injustices and tricks of statecraft. I used to dream, before I was too old, of begging my way home to Norway, blind as I am, and thence to Iceland and beyond, to that strange land where the Skraellings sail their lonely rivers in boats of birch-bark, without cities, perhaps without kings, or need to conquer and be conquered. I would like to have lived among them for a while, learnt their language and spoken to them of Christ. I fear, now, that this was one of the most wayward of a blind man's dreams.

(Ibid., p. 463)

6

ERIC GILL

There was dust and confusion in Blundell's School Chapel, with pews hurled aside and replaced by bags of cement. The Rev. Neville Gorton, the Headmaster, strode amidst the chaos of reconstruction, hatchet-faced and eager, earnest and eloquent. The changes being made were not, he would insist, a question of architecture or design. The work would be itself an act of worship, done by the boys themselves. What, we had to ask ourselves, is a Church for? It is to shelter a Christian Community assembled in worship. But what form does this worship take? It is essentially the gathering of believers round the communion table in fellowship with Christ and with each other. That, he would conclude, is the essence of the Liturgical Movement—the revival among us of the spirit of the primitive church. 'We must bring the altar to the people!' With vigorous gestures, the black gown floating behind him, the Headmaster would point as he talked, now to the chancel steps, now to the blocked east windows and now to the hammer beams of the roof. He would bring the boys to God or die in the attempt.

The voice was the voice of Gorton but the ideas came from Eric Gill (a hairy man), whose beard had recently wagged over the same scene and to startling effect. On the occasion of his first visit, early in 1938, Gorton had asked, 'Would the altar look better a few feet away from the East wall?'—to which the Catholic Gill had replied crushingly 'It doesn't matter where it would look better, the question is where it would *be* better, and where it will be better you will come to see that it looks better!' Completing his victory over a mere clergyman, Gill had then given the school a lecture on Christian altars. Back at Tiverton in May, he found the boys heroically at work and told them afresh that theirs was a liturgical, not merely an architectural reform. He stood in the midst and prophesied, looked about the chapel and saw that it was good. As masons, plasterers, builders and carpenters, the boys had thrown themselves into the task. Others did stonecarving and one was already at work on a statue, which began as Peter Blundell, turned into St Francis and ended finally as Jesus Christ. 'The right sequence!' was Gorton's comment as he strode out of the workshop, emphasising how important it had been in monastic life that the carving should be done by the monks themselves. Victim at Oxford of something called 'Greats', the Headmaster's knowledge of history was sketchy but his enthusiam was impressive. Born in 1888, the son of a clergyman, educated at Marlborough and Balliol, and ordained in 1914, he was Assistant Chaplain at Sedbergh from 1914 to 1934, going directly from there to the headmastership of Blundell's. He was a saintly man 'surrounded' as the Archbishop of Canterbury said, 'by gusts of the Holy Spirit'. He was often untidily dressed, seeming quite as unworldly as he was. Many of his holidays were spent hunting, on foot, across the Lakeland fells. He was a devoted husband and father and a member of the National Liberal Club. He was also genuinely interested in his pupils and was liked by many of them. The masters were perhaps more inclined to admire Mrs Gorton, who was a hostess of genius with the right word for everyone.

But how did I come to Blundell's in the first place? Elected to a Fellowship in 1935, I had spent another three years in historical research. For the first year I lived within easy reach of the British Museum and Public Record Office. At first from Oxted, and later from Crockham Hill, I travelled almost daily to London, returning with notebooks better filled and bibliography more complete. The eventual result was *Trade in the Eastern Seas, 1793–1813*, published by

Cambridge University Press in 1937. For the last two years, when I was actually writing the book, I was in residence at Emmanuel. I did some teaching and came to know something about how a college is governed and organised. I commanded the Infantry Unit of Cambridge University Officers' Training Corps. What I could not do was to make a career for myself at Cambridge. There was no scope there for the kind of history in which I had specialised. I had to consider, therefore, what I was to do next. If I gained some school experience, adding it to my doctorate and ex-Fellowship, I might be thought eligible, I imagined, for the headmastership of a public school. With this idea in mind I applied for the post of Senior History Master at Blundell's, Tiverton. I was appointed after interview and took up my duties in April 1938, inheriting a large History VI from my predecessors, one of them having been William Empson, the poet. Knowing my background as artist, the Headmaster relied upon me to strengthen his hand against the philistine and malcontent people who could not appreciate what he was trying to do. With the alterations in full swing, I was led to the Chapel and invited to comment. Were I to be considered as an embryo headmaster, secure of Gorton's support in the years to come, this was the moment of truth; the moment, that is to say, for falsehood. I failed, however, at the outset. Looking about me I came to the immediate conclusion that the chapel was too long; having been lengthened, I could see, as the school had grown. Pointing this out, I proposed a remedy. 'While it's too long,' I said, 'it would *seem* shorter if you built a choir screen towards the west end —between *that* window, say, and the next.' There was a moment of stunned silence, broken only by the distant sound of hammering. 'There *was* a screen,' said the Headmaster, 'and that is exactly where it was. We have just demolished it,' Another master talked hastily of something else and we moved towards the apse, where some heaps of marble chippings were to be turned into altar steps. 'You will notice that blocking the windows has actually made the chancel seem larger.' As between me and Mr Gorton all chance of a great friendship was virtually at an end.

Fate was against my becoming another Arnold, Sanderson, or Thring, but I retained—and indeed retain—a great interest in the public schools. Only perhaps six or eight of the larger schools can claim a medieval origin but through these the remainder have inherited one basically medieval idea. From a remote period the prosperous Englishman has thrown his sons out of the house at the age of seven. Whether they are really less tolerable than the youth of other countries could be a subject for research, but the fact of their expulsion is not in dispute. The medieval gentleman's son became a page, leaving home, at the age of seven; a squire (somewhere else) at the age of fourteen; a soldier eligible for knighthood at the age of twenty-one. The merchant's son followed a similar path as apprentice, journeyman and master. And to this day the ages of seven, fourteen and twenty-one represent, roughly, the successive phases of an upper-class education. Give or take a year, the age-group system lies at the root of English school tradition. Ideas have varied somewhat as to what boys shall do during their fourteen years of immaturity, but on one point we have been consistent and emphatic; whatever they do, they are not to do it at home.

While the public schools have an inheritance which is in some respects medieval, their buildings tend to date from about 1880. Their great period of expansion coincided with, and depended upon, the Industrial Revolution. Their development was conditioned by their relative accessibility, by rail, from the big cities and above all from London. But the same expansion was taking place overseas and a developing Empire took an increasing number of the parents to India, Africa and America. They no longer made a deliberate choice of a boarding school education for their sons, because there was, in fact, no alternative. But the public schools did more than care for those temporary orphans. They prepared them to go overseas in their turn, thus returning to the colonial environment in which many of them had, in fact, been born. To the British Empire the public schools were an inevitable and essential corollary. They also served to separate the boys from the girls, the point being that no future officer was likely to marry—or would even be allowed to marry—much before the age of thirty. This being so, there was every reason for a strict segregation combined with an insistence on the athletic as contrasted with the romantic side of life. The boy was given a cold bath and a cricket bat, the girl was given a pony, and there was to be no nonsense about marriage until he had reached the rank of captain or its civilian equivalent. Nor was this a matter of arbitrary decree, for the Empire could have been governed in no other way.

That the Empire was on the decline from 1905 is more obvious now than it was at the time, but its collapse after 1945 was apparent. And many people assumed that each declaration of independence would be followed by the closing of another public school. Far from that, the system gains strength every day, with more schools being founded and others striving for recognition. Why? Because the prosperous Englishman still throws his son out of the house at the age of seven or eight and more Englishmen than ever can now be described as prosperous. Apart from that, however, the public schools have been enormously strengthened by the impact, on the state system, of educational theory. Given a Ministry of Education and given a pack of pseudo-scientific pedagogical advisers, some fairly asinine schemes are likely to result. But the basic weakness of state education is not the result of particular follies but of general uncertainty. The parent seeks to plan for twenty-one years ahead. He wants to know beforehand the sort of college and school for which his son is to be prepared. The boy destined for the Army via Wellington and Sandhurst or for diplomacy via Winchester and New College is pre-conditioned beforehand for the sort of life he is to lead. But the whole system implies that the parent can know in advance what Cheltenham or Rugby is going to be like. Should any individual school suddenly become co-educational, changing the age of entry and altering the entire curriculum, the resulting chaos is carried back to the nursery and the maternity hospital. And this the average headmaster is made to realise. The parent who enters a boy for Sedbergh, Bedales, Downside or Bryanston has and needs to have a clear idea of what he is buying. The system becomes unworkable as soon as there is a doubt as to what will happen to the school over the next decade. And that is the precise point at which the state system breaks down. It is at the mercy of any illiterate who should become Minister of Education and of any lunatic to whom he may turn for advice. Assume, if we prefer, that all the official plans are intelligent and enlightened; the fact would remain that each year's plan could be different. So the state school lurches and sways through a fog of educational theory, driven this way and that by election results and popular pressures, while the public school offers something relatively dependable and known. Eton, the parents believe, will always be Eton.

This may sound theoretical but I was witness, as it happened, to its practical illustration. There was never more than one state-owned public school and that was the Royal Naval College at Dartmouth, where I went from Blundell's. There was even once, at Osborne, what was virtually a state-owned preparatory school; attended, like Dartmouth, by royalty. Now Dartmouth, besides costing about three times more than it need have done, was subject to a series of bewildering and inconsistent reforms. It was democratised and reorganised, abolished and restored. Short of being made co-educational, it was made subject to every political whim of the moment, with changes in everything from the age of entry to the objects of the curriculum. Even supposing that each reform was for the better—which no one has ever dared maintain—the fact remains that it died as a school and could only be revived as a technical college. In education, as in gardening, the frequency with which you change your mind is an evil in itself. I remember, during my military

A Law Unto Themselves

career, three changes in the regulations which prescribe the officer's salute with the sword. The fact that each was obviously for the worse sinks into insignificance beside the fact that they were made at all. Fussy amendments to the manual do no more than weaken the authority of the higher command but drastic reform in a school will incline parents to send their children elsewhere; not because the reforms are bad in themselves but because no one knows what is coming next.

For biological and logistic reasons which have never been thoroughly analysed, most public schools lie to the north and west of London and within a radius of about a hundred miles. Preparatory schools lie mostly in the opposite direction, fifty or sixty miles to the South and East, with a heavy concentration in Sussex, Surrey, Kent and Hampshire. While Seaford is generally recognised as the capital of the industry, there are two other important centres of production; one between Broadstairs and Folkestone, which is possibly declining, and the other round Newbury in Berkshire, which is probably on the upgrade. What research has been done would seem to suggest that public school locations represent a compromise between parental convenience at half-term and a desire to keep adolescents out of the London nightclubs. As for Etonians, these are mostly excluded from haunts of vice by the fear of meeting their parents there; a likelihood which, with Harrovians, becomes a certainty. Preparatory schools by contrast have to be within weekend motoring distance of London, near the sea or at least near a golf-course. Fathers want to combine duty with pleasure and for mothers the chief pleasure lies in parading a growing boy before such of their contemporaries as may be childless.

While most public schools lie within a hundred-mile radius from Charing Cross and are contained within an arc which extends from Canford to Oundle, there are some more remotely placed, like Ampleforth, St Peter's, Rossall, Shrewsbury and Sherborne. Among the most distant of these is Blundell's, Tiverton, almost as far-flung as Dartmouth itself.

ERIC GILL

Eric Gill

Its old buildings, completed in 1604, form a classic example of Elizabethan school planning but were deserted by the Victorians, who preferred to build on higher ground outside the town. It was in this 19th-century setting that Neville Gorton tried to apply the theories of Eric Gill, and all my early background should have inspired me to support him in the attempt. With my own inherited sense of craftsmanship and my own admiration for G. K. Chesterton, I should in theory have seen Eric Gill as a prophet and sage. I actually thought him a menace, and while I learnt something from Gorton about the way boys react, all I learnt from Eric Gill was how not to be like him. There was something, I'll admit, in his philosophy, but his general point of view was one I rejected then and reject to this day. Nor had I from the outset any sympathy with Gorton's religious enthusiasm. To bring his pupils to God might seem a reasonable object but it was not, basically, what the parents were paying him to do. His theory that compulsory attendance at chapel was wrong but that the boys must be made to go voluntarily, seemed to me outside the tradition of which he was the temporary custodian. As for Eric Gill, he had no business there at all.

Or is that entirely true? Eric Gill had something to teach and I have been at pains to discover what I may have learnt from him. He had a nonconformist background and had been apprenticed to a London architect. Coming under the influence of Edward Johnston, he turned from architecture to the carving of letters in stone, going on from that to sculpture in 1910. He became a Roman Catholic three years later, writing much thereafter on art and religion. At the time we met he had known Gorton for about four or five years. Basically he believed that our western civilisation is approaching its end and that 'industrialism will go down in blood and tears'. The effect of industrialism, meanwhile, is the divorce between art and life. For art, Gill would argue, is the skill of men, and a work of art is that which is made to fit its purpose—'the well making of what needs making'.

Put in another way 'we should hesitate to call that thing a work of art which served no purpose at all or, having a purpose, did not in the least degree serve it'. The objects of daily life are no longer made by men at all but by machines. The machine thus degrades the workman to the level of a mere tool, intellectually as well as economically enslaved. The artist, meanwhile, has been released from 'the degradation', as it has been called 'of having to make anything useful'. The contrast lies, as Gill put it between 'the artist, solely concerned to express himself' and 'the workman deprived of any self to express'. The result is to be seen in the dull machine-made products of the factory and the 'useless, non-didactic, non-anecdotal, non-representational' products of the studio which manifest merely 'the precious personality of the artist'.

So far, the argument may seem familiar enough, but Gill carried it a stage further, pointing out that the attempt to retrace our steps—as William Morris and his pupils had done, as my father tried to do—is hopeless. For we can work only in the world as we find it. 'You can't build a gothic or classic cathedral today,' said Gill, 'even in Liverpool, without making a fool of yourself.' Architecture, he maintained, in an industrial civilisation can be inspired only by industry. All we can build is a concrete box of decent proportions but devoid of ornament. To build Chartres Cathedral or the Parthenon demands not merely skilled craftsmen—such as we can neither find, nor afford—but a public able to appreciate what we are trying to do. But without manual skill of their own, people can appreciate nothing but mere entertainment. And the idea of the Leisure State, in which short hours of work are followed by the time for art and contemplation, must break down at the outset. For the art which is divorced from daily life and work is a hot-house plant of doubtful value; and the people whose work is mechanical would not appreciate real art even were they offered it.

Gill had, it is obvious, a message for mankind. In what form, however, did it reach Blundell's School? Gill's first point was that a public school offers an education which is confined, in practice, to books and physical development: to intellectual discipline and moral discipline. The mind is trained by words and ideas, the will mainly by games, and there is no time for *things*. The balance could be redressed only by wood-carving and pottery, metalwork and sculpture. Neville Gorton accepted this argument with religious fervour, the inevitable doubts being expressed more by Eric Gill than by him. 'But do middle class parents want things?' he asked, and, 'Does Mr Gorton want to set up a peculiar school for peculiar parents?' That may well have been the headmaster's ambition, but it ran counter to everything for which Blundell's stood. The basic fact, of which Gorton tended to lose sight, was that the school had been set up by somebody else and for purposes which that founder had been at pains to define. More than that, its value to the parents depended on their knowing in advance what it had to offer. To the country, Blundell's could promise a supply of dependable officers, courageous, literate and (above all) loyal. And what had Eric Gill to do with that? In the last resort he was not even on the same side. To a friend who spoke of joining the armed forces in 1939 Gill put the question, 'Is English civilization good or bad?' and worded his own answer as follows: 'I think it's foully bad and indefensible, but if you think it's good, then defend it.' It is fortunate, perhaps, that there were enough people who thought it just worth defending.

Eric Gill lived, as he knew, in a period of cultural decadence, but he failed to draw the right conclusions from his premise. For our first duty, if we are past the summit of our achievement, is to preserve all that is best in our heritage. Our second duty is to slow down the process of decline—which can, after all, last for centuries. And our third duty is to leave behind us, if we can, an imperishable legend rather than merely a mess in the kitchen sink. Towards such objects as these the public schools make a vast contribution. Plans for their reform are thus usually absurd. While there

is much to be said for founding new schools, like Bryanston
or Bedales, with differing and novel objects and ideals, there
is still more to be said for leaving the older schools as they
are. I, for one, was inclined to suspect that Peter Blundell
and Lord Chief Justice Popham were far abler men than
Neville Gorton or Eric Gill. Turning away from the chapel
reconstruction, which the boys (being boys) would obviously
never complete, I looked with more interest at the school's
original buildings, the school as known to Fairfax and Black-
more and Archbishop Temple. I urged that the Old Boys
should acquire the old school and give it back to the governors. And this, oddly enough, was what they did. But imagination dried up at that point and nobody could think what
to do next. The old school was finally handed over to the
National Trust, leaving Peter Blundell to turn uneasily in
his grave. No founder could have been more explicit about
what was to be done, but his was a heritage that men chose
to throw aside.

In a play called *The Housemaster* by Ian Hay, the eagerly
reforming headmaster is hastily given a bishopric (on the
North Circular Road) and his place is taken by the senior
housemaster as representing the school's proper tradition.
At Blundell's the story was different. While Neville Gorton
was duly made Bishop of Coventry, the claims of the senior
housemaster and obvious successor were overlooked. More
colourful characters were preferred, not always with the
best results, and the loyal and capable Mr Hotblack had to
watch them come and go. But that is not where the story
ends, for the new Bishop of Coventry was to have the sort
of memorial he would have preferred. It was not to be the
work of Eric Gill, who had died in November 1940, but was
very much in the Gill tradition. Enthroned in 1943, Gorton
found his cathedral destroyed by enemy action. He had the
chance, therefore, to influence the form in which it should
be rebuilt. A tidy story would require him to plan Coventry
as Gill would have had it, performing the play for which
Blundell's chapel had been the dress rehearsal. Actual events

were rather more confused, but the Very Reverend R. T. Howard (Provost) says of Gorton that 'his influence upon the reconstruction was very great'. It is clear, moreover, that he and the architect became close friends. It is Sir Basil Spence, moreover, who described him most vividly:

> He was also a great character and dressed in the most bizarre fashion. One got used to seeing him walking the streets of Coventry with a serene far-way expression, wearing a dilapidated overcoat, on his head a deer-stalker with flies hooked into it, heavy woollen stockings on his spindly legs, and if he didn't have on a huge undergraduate's scarf, one caught a glimpse of purple under his clerical collar. Sometimes he didn't even have a clerical collar, but an ordinary collar and tie.
>
> Basil Spence, *Phoenix at Coventry*, Fontana, 1964, p. 54. See also R. T. Howard, *Ruined and Rebuilt*, Cathedral Council, Coventry, 1962.

It would be wrong, nevertheless, to picture these two as agreeing firmly to reject the idea of a gothic replica. What killed any such scheme was the financial limit within which a quick result was to be achieved. The Reconstruction Committee had been given a million pounds by the War Damage Commission, 'for a plain replacement' and that was, initially, all or nearly all the money available. Eric Gill had argued against attempting to build cathedrals in either the gothic or classical style, but it was the financial argument which clinched the matter. No one *could* have built traditionally within the limits set; nor was it possible, for that matter, to execute even the 'contemporary' plans as originally drawn. More final still was the consideration of speed. The competition was announced in 1950, the building licence issued in 1954 and the cathedral virtually finished by 1962. To put this time-table into its proper perspective, we need to recall that work on Liverpool Cathedral began in 1904 and that completion by 2004 would be thought highly creditable to all concerned. It was to Sir Giles Scott, the architect of

Liverpool, that the Coventry folk had turned in the first place, but disagreements had forced him to resign in 1947. There can be no doubt, however, that a cathedral of his design would have taken a century to build, and that people today doubt whether their civilisation is to last that long. Our instinct is to finish what we want while it is still possible and before the cost has doubled again. To build a cathedral on the scale attempted at Liverpool is no longer thought really feasible. A 'contemporary' design was, therefore, the inevitable choice, welcomed by many for its boldness and vitality. Neville Gorton loved it from the beginning. There was to be no choir screen nor was there, as at Blundell's, the task of removing one. As for sculpture, Gorton solved the problem with the words, 'Epstein is the man for us.' Where he failed, however, was over the central position of the high altar. His plea was inevitably to bring the altar forward and hide the fidgeting choirboys behind it, but over this he was finally outvoted and overruled. The altar remained where the architect had originally placed it and Gorton himself died in 1955.

Was the saintly Gorton right in all his progressive thinking, and was I stupidly prejudiced in my opposition to many of his ideas? I still think that he was totally wrong and that Eric Gill was to blame for it. And the essence of his mistake was to believe that the trappings of novelty would strengthen the appeal of something that is essentially old. People whose beliefs rest upon a divine revelation which took place nearly two thousand years ago have the advantage of pleading consistency. They have been loyal to their creed over a long period of history. But to claim, in addition, that they are also abreast of the very latest fashion is nonsense. For one thing, it cannot be true. For another, it would weaken their case if it were. People who see the present age as decadent will turn naturally to the institutions which date from earlier periods; to ideas and methods associated with our centuries of highest achievements. For them the Church, including the Church of England, has the great appeal of its historic background and obvious stability. But those who believe in continual progress, with a brightly scientific future before us, will not in any case be devout communicants. If things of the present or future are what you admire, it is not to the established Church you would turn in the first place. Your religion, if any, would have to be of the very latest kind.

The absurdities of a modernised Christianity are the concern only of believers. But the attempts to modernise the monarchy, the older universities, the colleges and public schools are all plainly ridiculous; and never more so than in matters architectural. The attempt is continually being made to graft a 'contemporary' building into an old institution, and the arguments used are always the same. 'The Georgian builders thought nothing of building in their own style alongside the gothic buildings they had inherited. Why should we scruple to build in our own style alongside theirs?' The answer to that is that we don't have a style. All we do is governed by three factors; bad workmanship, lack of money and lack of time. In place of a style we have some engineering skill; enough to disguise, more or less, the narrow limits within which we have to work. And the time factor is perhaps the most important. The significant difference between the cathedrals at Liverpool and Coventry lies first and foremost, in the time people were prepared to spend over their respective tasks. The Liverpool folk of 1904 were prepared to spend a century over a building to stand for a thousand years. The planners at Coventry were prepared merely to spend a decade in constructing what they hoped might (possibly) last for a century. And that is the whole nature of decadence, whether in architecture or art; not merely an awareness of higher achievement in the past but an urgent sense of how short a time is still to go.

I have been concerned, from time to time, with building projects, and notably with plans for the University of Singapore, founded in 1949. There was discussion and disagreement over the layout and elevation but something was finally agreed, with perhaps five years allowed for completion. At that point (in 1954) I went on leave, flying with my family back to England. Having friends in Syria, the Livingstones of the Iraq Petroleum Company, we resolved to break the journey at Beirut in order to stay with them. Kindness itself, they made our visit memorable, partly by their hospitality, partly by taking us to see the ruins of Baalbek in Lebanon and the Crusader castle called Krak des Chevaliers. Baalbek is a Phoenician city by origin, standing on the edge of the desert, but the ruins there are Roman. Tall Corinthian columns suggest what sort of a city it must once have been. A day or two later we drove from Homs to Krak, finding the dry air of Syria a tonic after the humidity of Singapore. We climbed over that astonishing fortification and gazed from it over the surrounding country. There is little architectural similarity, heaven knows, between a Roman forum and a medieval castle. They differ as much in purpose as in style. But they have one point of resemblance and it lies in their builders' determination. The Roman officers and the crusading knights were alike in their resolve to have the work the way they wanted it irrespective of effort, cost or time. Alike in this and alike again in having come to a country so remote from home, they left behind them the traces of their tremendous strength. Seeing these ruins and reflecting upon them afterwards by the roadside in Lebanon, I remembered the planning committee back in Singapore. There came to me the sudden realisation that we were devoting to our whole project a fraction of the time and thought which the Romans must have given to a single pediment; a fraction of the care which the knights must have lavished in a single archway. Our relative failure was no longer, in my eyes, a probability. I could see now that it was certain.

7

ARTHUR BRYANT

Colonel Oliphant of the General Staff (Military Operations Division) had asked me to lunch with him at a rather obscure restaurant near Warren Street Underground Station. He more often lunched in the War Office canteen but he may have thought that an unsuitable rendezvous in the present instance. He might, after all, decide to appoint someone else; and with good reason. My military record revealed a chequered career. Commissioned more than twenty years earlier I had appeared fitfully in the Army List, with one moment in apparent command of a squadron of horsed cavalry and a more recent phase spent under intermittent shellfire behind Dover Castle. I ranked at the moment as Major, being a staff officer (Air II) to an Air Vice-Marshal. Still in the uniform of the Queen's Royals, I was involved at the time in the organisation and training of the R.A.F. Regiment. I had attended no staff course, however, and such staffwork as I had done was of the wrong kind and indeed in the wrong service. The Colonel ordered lunch for two and looked at me dubiously across the oilcloth. He seemed to be knowledgeable, diffident and infinitely polite. I felt at the time that he would have asked a more hopeful candidate to the Cavalry Club. I realise now that he was not a member. A slatternly waitress wiped the table and re-set the cutlery, presently returning with two plates of a nameless soup.

'One of our duties,' the Colonel was saying, 'is to keep the Admiralty informed of the military situation. Their heads of division meet each morning in the Upper War Room with

Cunningham or Syfret in the chair. We are present in order to put them in the picture from the War Office angle.'

'Very interesting, sir.'

'But you have to remember that the Admiralty works on an entirely different system, the very reverse of ours.'

'Different in what sense, sir?'

'Well, a telegram to the General Staff goes initially to a G.III, who suggests a reply to a G.II, who passes it, with or without amendments, to his G.I. He in turn advises the Brigadier, who takes the whole folder to the A.C.I.G.S. (O).'

'Where does the D.M.O. come into it?'

'He doesn't, not in wartime. But the point is that a signal to the Admiralty goes straight to the First Sea Lord, who makes his decision and passes it downward for detailed action at a lower level.'

'I suppose that the Admiralty must be a far smaller organisation?'

'Far smaller. Their system would be impossible for us. However, differ as we may in procedure, we get on well together in practice. We are also concerned, in our branch, with despatches; as also, sometimes, with Questions in the House.'

'What can you do about a despatch, sir? Apart, I mean, from acknowledging it?'

'Well, they can be a bit tricky. It is a question these days who can write one and to whom. Winston wrote a wonderful comment on that: "Let us not debase our currency. Otherwise we shall have despatches written after every trumpery foray." They are not to be published, of course, until the war is over.'

'No, I suppose not, sir.'

While we were talking there came the distant throbbing of an engine, something like that of a motor-cycle. Conversation died away in the restaurant, giving place to a strained silence as the sound approached.

'But even then it will be important to avoid giving offence to our allies or for that matter to the Air Force or Navy.'

'I quite see that. Rash things can be said in the heat of the moment.'

Our voices were the only sound apart from the throbbing noise; which now suddenly stopped. This was the signal for all the civilians present to dive under the furniture. The two officers in uniform continued to deal with staff duties and soup.

'They can indeed. But inaccurate statements are as bad, in a way, as the rashest comments.'

There was a deafening explosion and the whole building rocked. This was followed by the crash of broken glass and the thud of falling plaster. The restaurant was filled with dust, through which we could see the other customers emerging from under their tables. Somewhere behind the scenes a waitress was screaming hysterically. A waiter came in with a dustpan and brush. Another went to the door and looked to see where the bomb had fallen. With the addition of ceiling fragments, the soup was neither better nor worse.

'But you can't, surely, ask a general to alter his despatch?'

'Not exactly. But you can give him the chance to add a footnote.'

'Pointing out some fact, you mean, which he did not know at the time?'

'Exactly. So you can see that our work is both interesting and important; and requires, moreover, a sense of history.'

I agreed, noticing that the waitress had reappeared, with fishcakes and mashed potatoes. The Colonel said, 'Ah, good', absently, and then leaned forward as if to tell me something in strict confidence.

'That, by the way, was one of those V.1 things. . . .

'Oh, was it, sir?' I replied with the same nonchalance. 'Bad for the crockery.'

Whether because of my historical knowledge or my steadiness under fire, I was appointed soon afterwards to the General Staff. What impressed me, however, in that little scene was the change it had made in Britain's strategic position. I had been at Dover in January 1942, when the whole coastline bristled with weapons; when there had been a Division, to begin with, in the town itself. The situation was then very much what it had been in the time of Napoleon. There were the aircraft and there were the long-range guns on either side, but these had cancelled out, leaving the armies face to face but effectively separated by the Channel. On fine days we could see the opposite shore and would wonder, as we gazed, whether Hitler dared attempt the crossing. We took up position for battle on the nights which would best serve his purpose. George III's troops had done the same thing in the same situation. But by now, by December 1944, the whole situation had changed. With London itself within range of the V.1 and V.2, Britain was no longer an island. However much we might resent the fact, the British Isles had become, overnight, a part of Europe. To defend England we should have to deploy our troops (as we were later to do) in Germany.

I had reached this curious luncheon engagement by a rather circuitous route. In 1939, before the outbreak of war, I had applied for a vacancy on the civilian staff at the Royal Naval College, Dartmouth. I was interviewed there on the day that the submarine *Thetis* was lost. Very much on the recommendation of Vice-Admiral Sir Herbert Richmond, to whom I was personally known, my application was accepted. I saw this at the time as a backdoor entry to the Royal Navy or Marines. With war plainly imminent I believed that a Dartmouth master would readily achieve a naval commission. To enable a maritime historian to gain practical experience afloat would seem the merest common sense, making him the more valuable to the post-war Navy. But the Admiralty was a more compartmented organisation than I had realised, those concerned with war-time recruitment being wholly distinct from those responsible for peace-time education. I was not accepted for the Navy but told that my duty was to stay at Dartmouth. The result was that I was still there when France fell, applying alternately to the Army and the R.A.F. and it was September 1940 before the

Army re-posted me to my Regiment. Although once more in the Queen's Royals I was appointed to an Officer Cadet Training Unit and stationed at Colchester. The unit was moved bodily to the Isle of Man soon afterwards and then handed over to the R.A.F. for the training of its ground defence troops. When these were reorganised as the R.A.F. Regiment I was posted as Instructor to the Regimental Depot and then, as Major, to the Group responsible for training in ground defence. This promotion was the occasion for my marriage, my eldest child being born in December 1943. It was during the following year that I was called to this interview at the War Office and so to a point of vantage from which to study the developing conflict. For a time at least I knew what was happening.

As an historian I had specialised in the French Wars of 1793–1815. I was fascinated therefore, to see how history repeated itself. There was in 1939–43 the battle of the whale and the elephant, very much as in Nelson's time; the retreat from Europe, the failure at Dunkirk, the commando raids and the battle of the Atlantic convoys. Then there was the campaign in Egypt and the capitulation of the enemy, the occupation of Sicily and the landing in Calabria. Came finally the desperate invasion of Russia, a bid to conquer Moscow and the world. Even the old names recur in the more recent story—Dunkirk, Antwerp, Toulon, Cairo, Messina and Naples. Of this repetition historians were mostly aware, and none more so than Arthur Bryant. More even than Winston Churchill himself, Bryant found inspiration and encouragement in the comparison. Seizing a magnificent opportunity, he wrote a series of books which were to make him famous. *The Years of Endurance*, led to *The Years of Victory* and that to *The Age of Elegance*. And now the military posting that wafted me to Whitehall brought me into momentary contact with Britain's only professional historian; the only man I have known who could live and who has lived for years by the writing of history.

We have academic historians by the hundred; professors

and lecturers who research and publish. Some of them, like G. M. Trevelyan, have written for the public at large. Some are able, on or before retirement, to do that and nothing else. But Arthur Bryant has never held a professorial chair. He has been on the fringe of several universities, he is known in Fleet Street and has been seen round Windsor, but he has become neither teacher, editor nor court official. In an earlier age he would have been Lord Warden of the Stannaries or a Commissioner of Excise, with leisure for an unhurried authorship. Born too late in a country now so ill supplied with sinecures, he has written history for the general public, being more widely read perhaps than any of the professors. Free from that mixture of office-work and intrigue into which the academic life tends to resolve, he is a more genuine historian than many whose academic rank proclaims them such. No quadrangle bounds his vision and no unmarked essays crowd his desk. His freedom is limited, however, in another way, for the public is a harder taskmaster than the most redbrick of the modern universities.

Against 'popular' instruction, against the attempt to make knowledge available to all, and not merely to a circle of the erudite, it is easy to sneer. Bryant, like H. G. Wells and Lancelot Hogben, has had his share even of abuse. But jibes must fail in the presence of his actual achievement. He has succeeded where others would have failed; and what he could not accomplish his critics would not even dare attempt. Their criticism is apt in any case to miss its mark, being based on the assumption that what is popular must be wrong and that what is easy to read must be as easy to write. This sort of attack is not merely unfair; it is ill-informed. The popular author, like the lecturer at an evening class, labours admittedly under a disadvantage. The general reader, like the evening student, is seldom prepared to exert himself. He has done his day's work and expects, rather, to be entertained. But in the writing of history that condition does not necessarily conflict with the demands of scholarship. A book is not the less scholarly for being readable nor the more reliable for being dull. The difficulty lies elsewhere, in the time it takes to write. It was G. K. Chesterton, Bryant's predecessor in *The Illustrated London News*, who pointed out that solemnity is easy; that to write short jokes for *Tit-Bits* is more arduous than to write long articles for *The Times*. The same is true of history. To write the narrative may take even longer than to discover the facts.

This basic difficulty was discovered afresh by that leading historical novelist Mr C. S. Forester. After writing many of his Hornblower stories, combining a fictitious narrative with a largely authentic background, he was asked by a publisher to write a history of the naval war of 1812. His initial reluctance was beaten down by the mention of successively larger sums to be paid in advance, and he finally agreed to do as the publisher asked. But he told me afterwards that he would never try to write history again. 'Do you realise', he asked, 'that I had to read *fifty* other books before I could even *begin*?' I did realise it and have since thought that the process is akin to that used in translation from a foreign language. During Phase 1 we extract the meaning from the French text. In Phase 2 we put that meaning into English. But most people are content with Phase 1, feeling satisfied that the page is no longer French and failing to notice that it is almost as far from being English. Academic historians do much the same thing as a rule, organising the facts and probabilities into a sort of narrative but forgetting that the result is supposed to be a form of literature. The story may be there but it has never come to life.

To write the sort of history that can be classed as literature takes about twice as long as to write history for a learned periodical, and perhaps four times as long as to write a respectable fiction. So the problem, for the non-academic historian, is how to live for two years on the royalties of a single book. If the popular novelist can hardly expect more than that, the historian cannot expect as much. His obvious remedy is to alternate his more important works with others of smaller calibre; collected essays, short

'The Whitehall Game', as drawn by Thomas Derri[

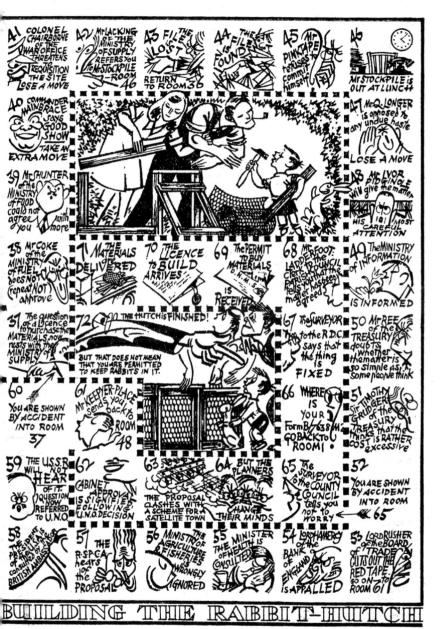

BUILDING THE RABBIT-HUTCH

blished by *Time and Tide*, 1946 (see page 116).

biographies, and books to meet public demand on a particular
occasion. This is what Arthur Bryant has done, but even
these lesser works have their value; partly because he takes
the trouble to master his subject and partly because he has
the courage to say what he thinks. Typical of his secondary
armament is his *Unfinished Victory*, a chronicle of the events
which led up to World War II. This cannot be called history
—no history was possible of events so recent—but it is an
extremely able commentary on that feverish age. And it has
also the virtue of courage. Publishing in 1940, Bryant still
maintains that the Germans had cause to be resentful over
the Treaty of Versailles. He still argues that the treatment
of Germany after 1918 was ungenerous, unjust and unwise.
This was no popular doctrine in 1940, nor is it much more
popular now. It is something, nevertheless, which needs to
be said.

As a weekly essayist, Arthur Bryant is a little dwarfed
by his predecessor. Could any author have assumed G. K.
Chesterton's mantle without feeling somewhat lost in its
folds? Even the most ephemeral of his essays will convey,
here and there, that hint of poetry which underlies his better
work. On the death of George V he wrote this memorable
passage:

> . . . On Thursday, January 28th, 1936, he was drawn by
> men from the Fleet through his capital with the pipes he
> had loved in life playing before him. The cold stones of
> St George's Chapel, Windsor, opened to receive him, and
> his body was laid among his fathers. Afterwards, as the
> mourners came out into the wintry air, they heard the
> living shouts of command and the clattering feet of the
> regiments that never die.

This is vividly written but it marks the point at which
conservatism breaks down. For the regiments which Bryant
thought immortal have since been disbanded or reduced
in strength. The Admiralty which directed our greatest
triumphs has been abolished. The palaces in London which

form the centre of our national life are overlooked by an American hotel. The dwindling clatter of the Household Cavalry is lost in the sound of the traffic, and Nelson from his column looks down upon the London offices of the colonies we have lost. Bryant remains identified, however, with the progressive outlook; with a belief in slum clearance and education. As a result perhaps of his work for the Conservatives and his association with the military planners of victory in World War II, he still looks to the future. He still sees freedom broadening down from precedent to precedent. Almost alone, moreover, among contemporary authors, he is in a position to tell the public what he thinks. There was a time when authors had some public influence: when the Press had room for the views of Bernard Shaw, H. G. Wells Dean Inge and Hilaire Belloc. No author has comparable influence today, but if there is a living writer with views to express and a platform from which to make them public, it is Sir Arthur Bryant. Of the periodical publicists he may not be the greatest, but he is certainly the last.

It is, however, as an historian that Bryant will be remembered. His main achievement begins with that first volume on Samuel Pepys, to which his book on Charles II forms, as it were, the prelude. *The Man in the Making* was followed at intervals by *The Years of Peril* and by *The Saviour of the Navy*. In resolutely tackling the last two volumes of his trilogy, Bryant was on new ground. To that labour which 'an historian (that would be exact) is condemned to', Arthur Bryant is no stranger. His interest in the past was awakened over forty years ago, not at Oxford (where textbooks, lectures and examinations made little impression on him) nor even at the Inner Temple, but in the muniment room of a country house in Cheshire. Since the days of his work on the Shakerley Manuscripts he has retained and developed not only a lingering affection for the great families but also an elaborate system of typewritten and pencilled notes, co-ordinated by such mysterious symbols as only he can understand. His text is not overladen with references but, if the scaffolding has been removed, the structure mostly stands secure. Each paragraph rests on the firm foundation of a card-index system by means of which any single assertion may be supported by a score of good authorities.

There were some critics who argued that the work had already been done. They preferred to give all the credit to Dr Tanner and to those other scholars for whom—as for Edwin Chappell—the diarist's complex personality had become a sort of obsession. This theory had some substance, as Bryant was the first to admit, but the standard biography remained to be written, its completion made no easier by the existence of so many conflicting theories. 'As to the compiler's province', wrote Evelyn once to his fellow diarist, "tis not easily to be imagined the sea and oceans of papers, treaties, declarations, relations and other pieces which I have been fain to sail through, read over, note and digest before I set pen to paper. . . .' Sir Arthur Bryant has noted and digested almost as much as he has sailed through before venturing into print. The Pepys volumes (apart from that still to come) were completed over a decade, their author and subject growing old, as it were, together. It would be hard to choose the best among them, the first making up in spontaneity for whatever is uneven in its form, the third making up in finish for whatever it has lost in vigour. The second, with its climax in the hitherto undiscovered story of the Popish Plot, might perhaps be thought the best. But all these books will live and the last of the series, when it appears, may yet prove best of all.

Following the completion of the Napoleonic trilogy in 1950, Bryant decided to take what he called at the time a busman's holiday. He would write a boy's history of England, fun to do and fun to read. His main handicap (as he soon discovered) was in knowing little outside the 17th and 19th centuries. 'All I knew', he told me, 'was what I had learnt at school and university—which was nothing!' Remedying his ignorance, he discovered that his history would be for adults and that it would run to five volumes at least and possibly six. Things are easier to get into than get out of, and Bryant now confesses ruefully, 'I have sentenced myself to hard labour—of the most exacting kind—for life!' Two volumes of this monumental work have now appeared, *Makers of the Realm* (1953), and *The Age of Chivalry* (1963). The delay over the second volume's appearance was not due to the author's struggle with medievalism but to his having turned aside to do something else, namely the editing of the Alanbrooke Diaries. He saw the task as urgent because Alanbrooke's name was almost unknown at that time outside the service. Were nothing done to correct this, a false picture would be perpetuated of how the war was actually planned. *Triumph in the West*, the second book based on the Diaries, did not appear until 1959. It was then that Bryant returned doggedly to the Middle Ages and to what would prove 'the best short history of the English people'. He was glad to find that the medievalists were more generous in their praise than the modern historians had ever been: the natural result, perhaps, of their being better scholars. More patronising were some of the journalists, who were and are apt to describe his work as mere 'popularization'. This sort of gibe has always infuriated Bryant, coming as it does from people who are totally ignorant of the work involved. Some idle remark about his prose being 'easy to read' stung him to make this comment in a letter to me:

> The truth is that it is only easy to read because, after I have spent years on first collecting and then arranging material—and how much there is no one who hasn't tried to write an up-to-date history of medieval England can have any idea!—I then rewrite and rewrite again and again until every unnecessary word has been eliminated and every sentence leads the reader naturally to the next and makes him want to find out what is in it. Most of my paragraphs have been rewritten and retyped at least a dozen and some of them twenty or thirty times over before it reaches its final form. For, as you had the

perception to see in that article you wrote on my work in *The Fortnightly*, this making of accurate history readable is an immensely laborious and artificial process. To write a single paragraph I have probably fifty or sixty closely typed folio sheets of extracts from books and documents in front of me, and all one does in one's first writing of it is to transfer a great mass of facts from one sheet (or rather many sheets) of paper to another, and the result, when typed, is utterly unreadable! It's usually only after many rewritings that a paragraph or chapter begins to appear like natural prose.

To illustrate the quality of that prose and to suggest at least one of the conclusions to which his studies have led him, here is a sample from *The Age of Chivalry* (Collins, London, 1963, p. 19).

It was a good time to live in for the fortunate so long as their fortune lasted, and a bad time for those whom fortune passed by. Yet, when all is said that can be charged against them, there was something that the Middle Ages had that we have not. Stand beneath the West front of Wells or Lincoln or under the tower of Ely and think. And then look at the piled boxes of concrete, glass and girder erected today with one object and one alone, and that the most transient of objects, and think again.

Considering Bryant's chief published works, one realises that they combine accuracy with an ease of style which leaves the reader unaware of the work involved. But this itself would hardly account for his success. People are seldom content with what is merely accurate and readable. In one thing, moreover, which might seem essential to popularity he is notably deficient, and that is humour. His strength is clearly not in wit nor in virulence, nor (except occasionally) in the beauty of his style. His strength lies in his appeal to what he calls 'the suppressed longings of the British race for colour and tradition and pageantry, driven for long beneath the drab surface of modern life'. He is, above all, a master of pageantry. He sees what he is describing and makes the reader see it too. Are we to trace this to his early upbringing at Court, or to later experience with the Greenwich Pageant, or to a marriage into the family which used to rule Sarawak? Whatever the cause, Bryant uses a pen as if he would be happier with a brush, or happiest of all, perhaps, in marshalling the characters on a crowded stage. Here is an example taken from a volume of essays called *Humanity in Politics*:

> For England is the land where contrasts blend and opposites, though irreconcilable, imperceptibly merge. Here, as in its sky and landscape, everything mingles and acquires a kind of unity. The contending armies seemingly about to clash are presently seen to be marching side by side. . . .

Note how the abstract statement quickly becomes a visual image. And then read this descriptive passage, the scene for which is in Northern England:

> . . . Waste places of charred green encompassed by stern boxlike dwellings, grey granite roads that climb between the factories and the eternal hills, pointed armies of marching roofs, moors that are blackened goldmines, dark jagged edges against the low fields and banners of smoke white and black in the cloud spangled Heavens, was there ever such a landscape to express the balanced battle, swaying now this way and now another, between man and nature?

If it is through his use of pageantry that Bryant draws his audience, he has at the end a message for them and one which an historian can properly convey. Believing as he still does in the future of democracy and in that education which is intended to make democracy possible, he yet sees much to value in an undemocratic but brightly coloured past and is anxious that what was best in it should be saved from destruction. We stand, he still believes, at the beginning of an age in which we may see a new society created, more egalitarian, more enlightened and hygienic than anything the historian can describe. But it is also an age of planned destruction in which town councillors and borough engineers compete in their eagerness to perfect or anticipate the damage which bombs may cause. The hatred and ingenuity of the enemy has nowhere kept pace with the havoc wrought by our own reformers. So that, while the newest power stations rise to confront our oldest cathedrals, the historian may be allowed, perhaps, to say his few halting words about the value of what is thrown aside. If he is to profess an object, other than the steadfast and exacting pursuit of whatever theme happens to interest him, he can surely choose no better aim than that.

Could I ever have followed in Bryant's footsteps, making a career simply as historian? He, after all, has shown that it can be done. For me, however, the task would have been more difficult. For I had specialised in maritime history, a subject as little recognised by the reading public as by the universities. The chair of Naval History at Cambridge had been quietly purloined by the imperialists, whose chair at Bristol was colonised from them in turn by the social scientists. As for the public at large, fiction readers would follow the fortunes of Hornblower, but not those of the men upon whose real exploits Mr C. S. Forester used to rely for his inspiration. Outside Dartmouth and Greenwich with their wildly uncertain future, there was no base from which a naval historian could operate and only a tiny ex-navy public to which he could appeal. I came nearest to success in this field when I joined the University of Liverpool. This followed my last brief period at the Royal Naval College, bombed out of Dartmouth and re-established for the time being at Eaton Hall, near Chester. Momentarily the turn of events had brought me back to the place where my parents had been born, and to the great country house beside which Victorian Chester seemed relatively unim-

ARTHUR BRYANT

portant. But the College was being drastically reformed and I could see no future for it or (in that context) for me. I applied for a teaching post at the University of Liverpool, one actually reserved for a specialist in naval and maritime history. The salary offered was ludicrous but it seemed possible that the lectureship might eventually become a Chair. Liverpool, with its tradition as a seaport, with its old-established shipping firms, with its nucleus collection of ship models and its local society for nautical research, was the very place in which to establish a school of maritime history. One could imagine a department at the University, a museum on the waterfront, some old wooden ship preserved in dry dock and a growing sense of local pride in all that the seaport has meant to Britain and the world. I made what I could of such opportunities as there were, but realised in the end that the task was impossible. While the Beatles were still to be born, the local Z-car police were already struggling to keep some sort of order among people whose main activity was in selling football pool coupons to each other. Bomb-damaged areas were the rendezvous for hooligans; and the task of reconstruction which might have been largely finished by 1947, was in Liverpool (as in London) the subject merely of an acrimonious argument; much being said and nothing being done. My attempt to make an historical centre at Liverpool involved a lecture room and library, both of my own providing. During the vacations I was trying to restore the house where my family was established, Elham Manor, between Canterbury and Folkestone, which dates (I suppose) from about 1350. I was compelled, therefore, to struggle simultaneously with two sets of local authorities. I thus came to know a great deal about city engineers and planners, rural district surveyors, plans and permits and timber control. I learnt as much again about the dishonesty of contractors and the incompetence of many architects. My experience was dearly bought but I could claim at the end to know what I was talking about.

A Law Unto Themselves

The result of my early friction with departmental ineptitude was *The Whitehall Game* (pp. 106–7). This was a version of Snakes and Ladders in which dice-throwing players move their counter so many squares on, encountering mishaps which send them perhaps as many squares back. Each player is assumed to be the intended builder of a rabbit-hutch. He applies initially to the Parish Coucil and is referred successively to the Rural District, the County Council and the Ministry of Health. Hazards are represented by the Army and Air Force, who want the land for something else, and by civil servants who merely lose the file. The decision is taken, in the end, by the United Nations, and passed down the line for executive action. The final winning square shows the hutch as triumphantly completed but yet another civil servant overshadowing it with hand raised in prohibition and the words 'But that doesn't mean that you can keep rabbits in it!' This was brilliantly illustrated by Thomas Derrick and published as a Christmas supplement to *Time and Tide*. We meant to place it on the market as a satiric parlour game, but no firm would make the venture, some fearing (they said) that it would make trouble for them in their relationship with government and municipal departments. I had previously written satirically about the crude and panic process which had placed most resident enemy aliens behind barbed wire in the Isle of Man—where I was stationed at one time during the war—but that story was never published. So *The Whitehall Game* may well represent my first public tilt at bureaucracy. It also contains the germ of an idea which blossomed finally as the Abominable No-Man. All this, however, was in the distant future. At the time I was chiefly aware of my failure at Liverpool. Unlike Sir Arthur Bryant, I had found no demand in England for the sort of history I had to offer. It was time to go, and on March the 5th, 1950, I embarked in the R.M.S. *Carthage* for Singapore. I doubted even then whether I should ever live in England again.

8

GERALD TEMPLER

Sir George Allen, Vice-Chancellor of the University of
Malaya, was giving a party. His house was on a hilltop,
overlooking the sea, the view extending to the Indonesian
islands to the southward. One's car circled the hill and left
behind the attap huts and stalls of the local villagers. The
hillside was alive with the noise of the cicadas, and native
dogs barked at the passing car. The house had an arched
colonnade on the seaward side, through which the sunset
could be seen when we arrived, the gold turning to purple
as night fell on Singapore. The host and his male guests
were in tropical evening dress, white jackets and black
trousers, the women in pretty frocks, and the Chinese
servants uniformed in white. It was a gay scene, with girls
laughing and glasses being refilled, stengahs and gimlets
being sipped, and formal introductions being made. Our
host was called to the telephone in the midst of it all and
came back looking so upset that the conversation died
away. 'I'm sorry to tell you all,' he said quietly, 'that the
High Commissioner was ambushed and killed this afternoon.' It had happened, he told us, on the road to Fraser's
Hill. Lady Gurney, he assured us, was still alive. Nothing
more was known and that, for the moment, was that. The
party went on but a little subdued, as people are still in the
presence of death.

I pondered afterwards on the meaning of the word
'romance', for the scene I have tried to describe was, to
me, supremely romantic. But what does that word mean?
A romantic scene is literally one too good to be true,

presenting incidents too theatrical for everyday life. There is
more to it, however, than that. For true romance involves
two other factors. With the exotic or picturesque scene must
go an element of danger and a sufficiency of domestic help.
The possibility of another ambush or riot was essential to the
plot. But so were the servants. For had the hostess reminded
her guests that they would be expected to help wash the
dishes, the scene would have ceased to be romantic. We
should not have resented the idea but we should have sensed
that a scene of fiction was being reduced to the level of fact.
That which is furthest from the romantic is the sordid, and
even the prosaic is a move in that direction. The romance of
British Malaya, itself a sort of footnote to the romance of
British India, was based essentially on domestic service, and
danger. In Singapore we had enough of both and there were
moments up country when the degree of risk seemed more,
even, than was strictly speaking necessary. Our lives were
romantic, therefore, and I feel to this day a kind of pity for
anyone who has never lived in the East.

I came to Singapore in 1950 and was plunged at once into
a life that was excitingly new and different. I had left behind
me in England a broken marriage, two children I should
not see again for a decade, a discarded career as naval
historian, a medieval manor house, and the books I had
collected (or written) over the last twenty years. I had
decided at the outset that my mission in Malaya should be
to create for the country the historical background which
its varied peoples might share. I found in practice that I had
other responsibilities as well; those involved in forming a
new university and those arising from the Colony's emergent
nationality. Background to all this activity was a civil war
(as we have seen) and a ferment of political activity.

The choice of a successor to Sir Henry Gurney fell to the
Prime Minister, then Mr Winston Churchill, who had a
crucial decision to make. Advised by Mr Oliver Lyttelton
(now Lord Chandos), the Secretary of State for the Colonies,
Churchill concluded that it was essential to unify the

command. So far the civil war had been waged by the High-Commissioner, as controlling the police, in partnership with the Commander-in-Chief, who controlled the Army. Co-operation had in fact been extremely poor, the police accusing the soldiers of careless talk, the soldiers suspecting the police of treachery. Towards gaining a combined effort the first step was to subordinate all security forces to a military High-Commissioner. The choice fell on General Sir Gerald Templer, at that time G.O.C. Eastern Command, but previously Vice-Chief of the Imperial General Staff, and at one time Director of Military Government in Germany. Having served with Alexander and Montgomery, he was a fighting soldier of great experience, but he had added to that a knowledge of political affairs. He had the further merit of being junior to such generals as Slim and Nye, who would have had to command the Far East Land Forces were they to be appointed at all. He was at this time, however, comparatively unknown, having been no more than a Divisional Commander when a wound in Italy ended, for the time being, his career in the field.

In making a comparison of the British efforts in the two World Wars the historian is bound to observe that successful diplomacy before 1914 was the prelude to a remarkably unimaginative military leadership; whereas the lack of foreign policy before 1939 was redeemed by a subsequent brilliance in both strategy and tactics. We excuse the earlier generals in so far as they were misled by the French, who lacked any recent military experience, but that was not the whole of the story. For the generals of the two World Wars did not even have the same racial origin. After our experience of Scottish generals in 1914–18 we developed an unconscious prejudice against them. We also seem to have realised that the best way to exclude the Scots is to call in the protestant Irish. Our best generals of World War II were Irish almost to a man, with essentially the same background as the Duke of Wellington. There was nothing in these tactics to preserve us from Scottish Prime Ministers and Archbishops, but it saved us from the worst in 1939–45. Among these Irish leaders Gerald Templer was one of the most successful; combining, as did the others, a gift for leadership with a sense of style. Tough and resilient, aggressive and yet cautious, energetic but sensitive, Templer is among the great soldiers of his day.

I am not one of those who regard the war years as a wasted part of my life. Far from that, they were essential to all that I have tried to do since. It so happens, nevertheless, that I owe least to the officers under whom I served and most to those I knew afterwards in Malaya. My wartime seniors taught me a great deal—not least the Air Vice-Marshal who told me that his letters were to have 'no adjectives'—but others were to teach me more. With Templer I was associated only briefly as his biographer, but the impression was immediate and lasting. There are generals I have known better and liked as much—Frank Brooke being certainly one—but Templer's impact was (and is) of a peculiar kind. The celibate Knights of the Temple—to the misconduct of one of whom the Templer family must presumably owe its origin—fought under a standard which was half black and half white, suggesting a contrast between their conduct towards Infidel and Christian. They were supposed to unite the gentleness of the lamb with the strength of the lion, the patience of the hermit with the heroism of the knight. True to this possible ancestry, Sir Gerald presents the same sort of contrast; a brutal directness and intolerance of language united incongruously with a generous enthusiasm and a love for nature, people and art.

To understand Templer's impact on Malaya we need to realise, first of all, that he was a soldier assuming what had always been a civilian office. We must also remember that Malaya had been conquered by the Japanese, remaining under their rule from 1942 to 1945. During that period most of its former administrators were in the prison camp, scarcely expecting to survive their treatment. Released and rehabilitated, they were sent back to a duty which involved, from 1948, the attempted suppression of a communist revolt. Knowing the country, the people, the language and customs, the men of the Malayan Civil Service numbered about 320; of which total, making allowance for sickness, leave and early inexperience, some 200 effective men might be available at any given moment. In peacetime this was or had been a sufficiency of talent. While these officers were not of the intellectual calibre of those appointed to the I.C.S., it would be wrong to regard them as rejects. They were men prepared for work in less civilised surroundings and among peoples more varied even than those of India. Some of them were very capable indeed, well suited to the responsibilities of government. For fighting a civil war their qualifications were less obvious, for their immediate background was one of defeat and captivity. And whereas defeat in Britain had been followed by the exhilaration of victory, the British in Malaya had known only defeat, followed not by victory but by an abrupt and almost inexplicable collapse of the other side, due entirely to events elsewhere. In these circumstances the wonder is not that their morale was low but that it was as high as it proved to be. They showed no lack of courage but they were psychologically more prepared to die fighting than to beat the other side. By 1951 the situation was 'very grave', with resignations at the senior level and an obvious decline of confidence.

Even against this gloomy background, the members of the M.C.S. were inclined to resent the choice of an Army High-Commissioner. As against the terrorists in the jungle merely military methods had already failed. The biggest operations, with artillery and bombers and warships, with infantry deployed by the thousand, had always produced the least result. It was far more a problem, they thought, for the Special Branch and the Secret Service, for the Chinese Secretariat and the Information Department. These soldiers were too clumsy to achieve anything. They moved so noisily in the jungle that the enemy always had warning of their approach. As for the generals, they might be well-intentioned in their way, but their plans were always too obvious. The subtle Chinese were always a jump ahead of them. Remember the generals of 1942! And what could this man Templer have learnt at Wellington, at Sandhurst or in the Royal Irish Fusiliers? He was the man, it was rumoured, who had sacked Adenauer from his office as Burgermeister. His period of office in Malaya would mean, surely, the rule of the jackboot, with soldiers everywhere and the civilians pushed aside. And what good would it do, all this shouting and bullying, all this heel-clicking and saluting? It was not that kind of war. There was also, remember, the political side. Malaya had already been promised its independence. There was to be a democratic constitution, a replacement of the British administrators, a development of a party system and the setting up of all that the British associate with the independence of a former colony. What could an Irish soldier know about democracy? On this last point we could fairly ask, in passing, what the M.C.S. knew about it either. It remains a curious British assumption that colonial civil servants, who have never canvassed or even recorded a vote, are the ideal evangelists of a democracy in which they cannot possibly believe. Be that, however, as it may, the civilians were apprehensive about Templer from the start. Neither he nor his civilian Deputy, Sir Donald MacGillivray, had been in Malaya before. They knew nothing of the oriental mind, nothing of the Far East at all. It would be a case, they felt, of a bull in a China shop; and it was they, of course, who would have to sweep up the broken porcelain.

While the last paragraph may fairly summarise a not unreasonable point of view, we have to recall that other people felt differently. The planters, the miners and business men were impatient with the administrators and were demanding action. Their wives and children were living in a state of siege. They themselves were being ambushed and many of their friends and neighbours had already been killed. Were the planters to lose heart and sail home, the

GERALD TEMPLER

country's whole economy would collapse. It was vital to their morale that something drastic should be done. As for the non-communist Chinese, they are not as subtle as we often imagine. Where they differ from the European is in being more realistic. Confronted by a battlefield or a race-course, they seek, first and foremost, to spot the winner. To be on the losing side, they feel, is neither dignified, profitable nor even safe. It is for this reason that diplomacy is usually lost on the Chinese. If they foresee your defeat, you are wasting your time. If they anticipate your victory, it is they who will be trying their diplomacy on you. The vital thing is to give the impression that your success is certain and that your opponents are merely unlucky. This cannot be done, however by a mere play-acting. You need to have a real confidence in your own real abilities. It must be made clear from the start that you simply cannot lose.

Templer's first official conference has become a legend. Summoning all senior officials to Kuala Lumpur within a few days of his arrival, he found himself confronting an anything but friendly audience. As he said over two years afterwards:

Believe me, to be confronted by row on row of the M.C.S., their upturned faces registering that mild in-credulity which is all they permit themselves by way of comment, could well reduce an amateur High-Commis-sioner to that state of incoherence when he has to be led twittering from the rostrum.

(C. Northcote Parkinson, *Templer in Malaya*. Donald Moore, Singapore, 1954, p. 18)

Far from incoherent, Sir Gerald asked, instead, a single deadly question: '*What is being done about archaeology?*' With six words he had routed his potential critics. What-ever the subjects upon which they had briefed themselves, archaeology was not one of them. Nor was this mere show-manship, for Templer (as it soon transpired) had been collecting Chinese porcelain for the last twenty years and

had learnt about Sung pottery from the great Eumorpho-
poulos himself. It also appeared that he was something of
an authority on miniatures. . . . To sum up, the theory that
he was a simple, blunt regimental soldier broke down in the
first few days. Whatever else he might be, he was clearly
not that.

In conversation with me a year later Templer referred to
his early encounters with the Malayan Civil Service and
agreed with me that some of its representatives were not
quite up to the mark. 'No wonder,' he added, 'after all they
have been through.' But he went on to speak very highly
of the M.C.S. as a whole. 'Most of them did a splendid job
of work for me, and I was and am deeply grateful to them.'
There were stories current at the time of what he had said
to the less outstanding among them; stories which Templer
describes as mostly untrue. The fact remains that these
anecdotes served a good purpose, raising morale and tending
to show that the situation was being brought under control.
And while Templer is generous, in retrospect, about the
way in which he was served, some of the good work was
done by men he had inspired and not a little by men he had
terrified.

Having dealt with the M.C.S., Templer showed another
side of himself to the planters and miners; as also to the
Chinese. On them he used the technique of personal contact,
as practised by Montgomery, by Nelson, and by nearly all
great leaders back to the battle of Megiddo and the Siege of
Troy. Lady Templer, meanwhile, was practising the same
and other arts of persuasion in a different direction. It was
she who started the Women's Institute in Malaya, inducing
the women of different races to mix together on friendly
terms. She worked as hard for the Red Cross, for St John's,
for the Girl Guides and for every activity in which women
could be involved. 'She worked the skin off her fingers,'
says Templer, 'all the time we were out there—she worked
herself out.' This was obvious to everyone at the time, her
final monument being the T.B. Research Hospital which

was named after her. She travelled almost as much as her husband, whose stamina became a legend.

Leaving MacGillivray to keep goal at the seat of government, leaving Miss Jane Templer (when her mother was absent) to control King's House, Sir Gerald began to tour the country with an energy which left other folk appalled. 'Working at this speed, in this climate,' said men of experience, 'he will last about six months.' They were wrong. He did not collapse for over two years. And for much of that time he was in constant movement, going always as it were towards the sound of the guns. Whenever there was an 'incident', whether a train derailed or a factory burnt down, a planter ambushed or a village attacked, there was an even more frightening sequel. Next day and perhaps at daybreak there would be a commotion as a squadron of armoured cars screamed up the road and came to a quivering standstill amidst a cloud of dust. Out jumped no captain or subaltern but the High-Commissioner himself. And he wanted to know, there and then, where everyone had been and what everyone had done and why. He fairly exploded, in language totally unprintable, his occasional word of approval having, by contrast, the effect of a secular canonisation. The story goes that on one occasion the man to blame was obviously the District Officer, who had failed before in exactly the same way. He stood there among the others, apparently unnoticed, while the storm was at its height. At last the High-Commissioner turned back to his car. Pausing then, as if struck by an afterthought, Sir Gerald suddenly turned on the D.O. and said 'As for *you*, as for YOU, if I ever so much as hear your name again, I shall come back and . . .' the rest of the sentence being lost (perhaps fortunately) in the roar of the engines. A moment later the squadron had gone, leaving the local authorities to stare at each other through the subsiding dust.

It was stories like this which, true or false, gave planters the assurance that their safety was deemed important; that government was concerned about them. As for the officials, they were bound to ask themselves, 'If *this* were to happen tonight, and Templer were to arrive here tomorrow, what should I have to say? What should I be doing now? What have I left undone?' Men frightened by Templer became more frightening to their underlings and less nervous about the enemy. There were worse things (they found) than being ambushed. So it was that the impact of personality passed right down the chain of command, being felt by the watchman at the godown, by the sentry at the gate. As from the minute of Templer's arrival there was no excuse for anything. And the realist Chinese could sense the change in atmosphere. Perhaps the British had still to be reckoned with! Perhaps there would be no repetition of 1942? Now might be the moment to increase one's subscription to the Y.M.C.A. and curtail that other contribution, paid secretly through several intermediaries, which went to the Communists. . . . Malaya might have a future after all, and not merely as a province of China. There is no space here to discuss the details of jungle warfare or of Templer's contribution to the victory that was finally won. What does have to be recorded is the effect of his personality, that curious mingling of apparent brutality with cultural refinement; the military vigour with which he will suddenly express a quite unmilitary idea. In the midst of a discussion with me about the school syllabus, he suddenly said, 'Do you realise that these bloody children have no fairy-stories? Think of it—*no fairy-stories!*' The result of this chance remark was the publication of *Malayan Fables* (Parts I and II) by my wife, and *Heroes of Malaya* which was produced as a joint effort, both still very much in circulation. He sparked off a host of other ideas, from the National Museum to the Forum Club, from the National Parks to the Arts Theatre Group. There was also, and always, his interest in antiquity. To that opening question 'What is being done about archaeology?' I was eventually among those in a position to reply. And I could have answered 'A great deal!'

Templer's influence lingered for years after he had left the country, and nowhere more lastingly than in the trouble-some new village of Yong Peng. The Chinese there were always suspected and often proved to be in collusion with the terrorists. Templer therefore visited the place repeatedly, addressing their elders in vitriolic fashion and imposing the necessary penalties from the strictest curfew to the tightest control of rice. Things slowly improved but when he was about to leave Malaya the Village Council asked how they were to manage without him. To this Sir Gerald replied that if they wrote, he would always answer. A correspondence went on, in fact, for years, and whenever he was promoted or appeared in the Honours List, the telegram of congratulations from Yong Peng was always one of the first to arrive. This did not mean, however, that the village was out of trouble. Far from that, the District Officer was at his wit's end over the backsliding that went on. He imposed all the old penalties afresh and made life as unpleasant for the community as the law would allow. The villagers did not seem at all concerned. Nettled by this, he said to the elders: 'You don't seem to mind much! And yet what I've done is just what General Templer did—and you *minded*, then!' 'Yes,' they replied with great relish. 'But HE used to say such dreadful things to us as well!'

Of my time in Malaya, three scenes will always, I think, remain with me. The first concerns the genesis of Parkinson's Law. Some socialist politician was quoted as assuring a Conference on Adult Education that the Malayan government departments were all understaffed and overworked, and that suggestions to the contrary came only from people who feared an increase in taxation. I felt moved to reply in an article under the title 'The Educationists and the Pyramid'. After deploring the use of publicly financed adult education as a vehicle for party propaganda, I went on to question whether overwork is a symptom of understaffing:

This is not necessarily true and the general public, in assuming (without inquiry) that Government departments

127

are probably overstaffed, shows a vague awareness of the fact.

What the businessman, in particular, grasps is that while he himself has an economic motive for keeping his staff small, the civil servant has an economic motive for making his staff large. It may all be traced to the fact that consequence and salary in the Civil Service ultimately often depend upon the number of one's subordinates.

Mr Pending, we will suppose, has run the third branch of the Hesitation Department for some years. He finds that his work is increasing to such an extent that he rarely leaves his office before seven in the evening. He feels overworked. He could now go to his chief (Mr Ivor Pigeonhole, C.M.G.) and propose that a fourth branch should be created and half his present work given to a colleague of the same rank as himself. But this he will never do.

For the better plan, from his point of view, is to propose that the third branch should be divided into sections A and B, the one under Mr Intray, the other under Mr Outray. This gives Mr Pending a higher status and possibly a higher salary but, as he still makes all the decisions, he works as long hours as before. In fact, his hours are longer for he has now the added staff problems of leave and sickness and office space. He now seldom leaves before 7.30 p.m. and Messrs Intray and Outray dare not leave before him. They complain of overwork and Mr Pending, C.M.G., agrees that there seems to be a case for an increase in the establishment. This ends in Mr Intray having two assistants, Mr Cypher and Miss Nought, while Mr Outray (who in fairness can have no less) is now assisted by Miss Zero and Mr Nothingness. So the pyramid rises.

Meanwhile, however, Sir Always Pending, K.C.M.G., is practically collapsing from overwork. Nor are the rest idle; far from it. A large staff creates work for itself by a law of its own nature which has yet to be plotted on a graph, and it grows still larger by a progression best shown as an ever-steepening curve. The rule is that to raise the summit of your pyramid you must widen the base. But the impartial observer is apt to wonder whether the pyramid is anyway, the right shape.

I had there the essential idea of Parkinson's Law and there was nothing to prevent me revealing it to the world in 1951. If I did not do so it was because my concern was then with Malaya, with the difficulties of creating a new country. Overstaffing was the least of these, the immediate problem being to fashion some sort of government against the background of a civil war. So far as that was concerned, I could do no more than make suggestions. But I had a direct responsibility for giving the new Malaya its history and its historians, and some share in creating its new university, from which its future leaders would presumably emerge. I travelled and lectured, organised and broadcast, and was serving at one time on no fewer than thirty-two committees. It was not until 1955 that I thought again about the way in which administrators make work for each other. I find it easier to explain my neglect of this subject than my renewed interest. The facts, however, are these. Taking local leave in June, I travelled to Bangkok, where I was present, as it happened for a total eclipse of the sun. Travelling there by rail I had to change trains at Haadyai, where I had a long argument on the platform with a Thai Brigadier. I complained to him that the Malayan communists had their main headquarters on Siamese territory. This he flatly denied but we could neither of us make any impression on the other by argument. In point of fact, the communist leader, Chin Peng, posted a missive from Haadyai itself on, I think, the following day. We might have collided with him on the railway platform while we argued. I was denied the chance of meeting the brigadier again, however, and my business otherwise went according to plan; the arrangement being that I should join up with my wife and child at the Kuala Trengganu Rest House. This I did and we were on a seaside holiday there for five days, from June the 25th to the 30th. During that time I wrote the essay which came to be published as Parkinson's Law. The background to that writing was the Trengganu shore facing the Sea of China, frequented by fishing craft of the most dramatic design, sometimes with sails set against the morning sky, sometimes drawn up at sunset on the palm-fringed beach. These are pictures which remain with me still, a reminder of much that I loved in the East. By July the 4th we were back in Singapore and caught up again in a round of activities. It was not until September the 19th that the typed article was finally posted to the *Economist*. There were a thousand other things to do, culminating in an Historical Exhibition and Pageant and the fate of that article was hardly noticed at the time. I could not know that it was destined to change my whole way of life.

In 1957 Vernon Bartlett went on leave, inviting me to take over the duties, in his absence, of correspondent for the *Manchester Guardian*. This enabled me to be present, as a reporter, at the Malayan Independence celebrations of August the 31st, 1957. The programme covered the Declaration of Independence, the Historical Pageant, the Garden Party, the installation of the Paramount Ruler and the State Opening of Parliament. Much that was impressive was mingled with much that was amusing, but almost the most memorable moment, for me, was a glimpse I had of Sir Gerald Templer. He had left Malaya in 1954 and I had seen him afterwards in London, where he was convalescent after the illness which brought his Malayan career to an end. By 1957 he was a Field-Marshal and Chief of the Imperial General Staff. As such, he was invited to witness the day of Independence which he had done so much to bring about. The morning began with a rainstorm which delayed the proceedings for perhaps an hour. In the official seats of the new stadium people moved around, chatting. It was then that I came across the C.I.G.S., resplendent in full uniform, with baton in hand. He was the centre of a group of Malays and Chinese, talking animatedly and moving jerkily about as he always does, limping from an old wound and as restless as ever. One of his Chinese friends led up to him a child aged perhaps three. In an instant the Field-Marshal, with plumes and sword and baton, had knelt down in order to shake hands with the little boy. There are few other men living who could have made that gesture without a trace of self-consciousness. Few others there, perhaps, could have made it at all.

One of my last recollections of Malaya is concerned only indirectly with Templer. It is relevant, nevertheless, to all that he had tried to do. We had formed the University Archaeological Society in 1953, its field activities beginning that year at Johore Lama. There was a terrific response among my lecturers and pupils and it was an inspiration to see them at work together with all racial differences forgotten. If my wife and I failed to visit Angkor, it was because we were seeking buried cities in Malaya itself. What is more, we found them. In March 1958 we had two expeditions in the field, one on the lower features of Kedah Peak and the other (for beginners) at Malacca. When I went to visit the Kedah group, led by Alistair Lamb and Wang Gung Wu, I found them at once jubilant and disconsolate. They had discovered a buried temple with its walls intact to a height of five feet. They had removed the jungle which had concealed it, stripped off the soil and revealed, finally, a stone casket as used for the burial of a king's ashes. The temple had evidently been the royal mausoleum, overlooking the city of which the plains below still showed some trace. Hardly had this discovery been made, however, when a battle developed across the site between a Squadron of the R.A.F. Regiment and some thirty terrorists known to be in this area. Alistair had withdrawn his expedition to a village on the jungle's edge, being warned not to return. There could be mortar fire, he was told, and the alerted Home Guard would all be trigger happy. I had to see the place nevertheless and we made our way there one evening against all better counsel. It was a slightly eerie experience but I shall never forget the temple site (now a national monument) nor the students' sense of achievement. It was the history of their country which we had been trying to unearth, and it was they whose hands had done the actual work. For me and for my colleagues this was the reward of several years of organisation and effort. From the formation of the Society to the raising of the funds, from the training of the students to the air reconnaissance which had pinpointed the site, we had been hoping for just such a success as was finally ours. For Alistair, a purist in matters of scholarship, that was reward enough in itself. But for Ken Tregonning—to whose initiative the Society could trace its birth—and also to me, the adventure was more important in another way. These students, men and women of the new Malaya, could feel that they had made their own contribution to its history and culture. As had been our policy in the actual teaching of history, we had not tried to give them the answers ready made. All we had done was to lead them to the sources and say 'Now tell the story for yourselves.' There is no space here for any real account of their response. But if there is hope for Malaysia, surrounded as it is by open enemies and dubious friends, it is because there are young people there of this type, ready for adventure and responsive to leadership. They may feel, moreover, looking back, that men like Sir Gerald Templer—that men, for that matter, like Sir Stamford Raffles, who founded Singapore—were Malayan patriots and more loyal to the concept of Malaya than many since who have given tongue against 'colonialism'. But even these most intelligent men and women, my former pupils and later colleagues, owe more perhaps to Templer than they will ever know.

9

LEE KUAN YEW

Among the more heroic figures of the 20th century are the leaders of nationalism in territories which formed a part of the British Empire. They stand magnificently silhouetted against the sunrise, pointing the way to independence, prosperity and progress. They stand ready to mount the sort of pedestal erected for George Washington and Simon Bolivar; for all, indeed, who have dared all in the cause of Freedom. But the invariable rule which governs these contemporary rebellions is that the door broken down with dramatic violence was never locked in the first place. People do not rise against tyranny as such but against the rule which is plainly tottering. In the British Commonwealth the race has been between colonial governors and native politicians, the latter trying to seize beforehand what the former have obviously been told to give away. Nor are these heroes of independence being merely ungrateful, ungracious or dense. Their local popularity rests upon their defiance of authority, so much so that the Colonial Office must sometimes strengthen their hand by offering a token resistance, something they can appear to vanquish. But the British prefer, in general, to leave with an air of generous concession rather than one of panic surrender. For they may want to trade after they have ceased to rule.

As between colonial governors and their Asian or African ministers there is more mutual regard than is often allowed to appear; the sort of relationship we might expect to find between people whose educational background is the same. Veiling this basis of understanding, however, is the public

133

legend of anti-colonial heroism, and behind that again an impersonal and generalised resentment; the hostility felt towards the white man as such, quite compatible in practice with the politician's liking for every Englishman he may actually have met. It is against this background of strangely conflicting emotions that our former colonies plod their way unsteadily towards a precarious independence. The pattern, moreover, of their political progress is now becoming familiar. There is a standard procedure and it begins with a period of tutelage. The embryo native government takes virtual control of an administrative machine with the L-plate prominently displayed. An embryo Prime Minister takes the wheel and is told what route to follow, from Responsible Government to Universal Suffrage, from Electoral Registers to the Day of Independence. As the Parliamentary pattern is to be followed, the Prime Minister must be guided initially by Harrovians and Wykhamists who are assumed to be experts in democratic government. If there is an objection to this form of backseat driving it might lie in the fact that these colonial officials know practically nothing about democracy and regard it, anyway, with an ill-concealed loathing which all subsequent events are likely to justify. The first Prime Minister will probably have been coached for a political career, nursed by the British as the sort of native they would like to see in power. He seeks to disguise this fact by displays of calculated insolence. Ignoring these, his opponents describe him as a colonialist puppet. Tagged with this fatal epithet, he is thrown out at the second General Election, his successor being somebody who was jailed once for sedition; and several times, possibly, for commercial fraud. This Martyr in the Sacred Cause is ejected in turn by the leader of a party which is largely Communist. Following that leader's death in rather mysterious circumstances, an avowed Communist, the previous Home Secretary, comes into power and the British civil servants turn to each other (at Torquay) and say 'I told you so!'

The known Communist's chief political asset lies in the accepted belief that he could never, never have been the British choice. Feared as a Communist in a situation where fear is vital to success, his continuing popularity (such as it is) rests upon his reputation for applying the colour bar in reverse. However dubious his background, he is not, nor has he ever been, a member of the Cricket Club. Stories to account for his bitterness are in circulation, that he was kept out of Rotary, that his mother had an affair with an R.A.F. Flight-Lieutenant, and he may well have fostered these rumours himself. They serve, at least, as a guarantee of his anti-colonial character. His tenure of office, however, and his actual survival rest squarely upon his being as far to the left as is possible. No one still more extreme can plausibly brand him as a crypto-conservative. It is, after all, the generally accepted rule that the moderates must fail in a time of revolution, that the Jacobin must eternally supplant the Girondin, and that the pink of the evening sky must always turn to scarlet as the sun goes down.

The story of self-governing Singapore ran true, at first, to this classic pattern. The Conservatives, called here Progressives, who had been coached for office, were annihilated at the General Election of 1955, and David Marshall took office as leader of the Labour Front. He could scarcely have done so without the Governor's action in nominating two more of his party, men who had not even stood for election. With a small and uncertain majority, the first Chief Minister began what was to prove a brief but picturesque period in office. David Marshall was (and is) an Asian lawyer of Jewish descent, known for his eloquence as defence counsel in criminal cases. His assumed surname and his social habits made him seem more European than he actually was, but there could be no doubt that English was his first language. A man of impulsive generosity, his approach to politics was essentially emotional. He had seen himself as Leader of the Opposition, champion of the lower classes against the Progressive capitalists whom he and everyone else expected to see in office. All his courtroom technique could have been thrown into passionate pleas for the oppressed poor. He was not himself to be classed among them, for he was far wealthier than most of his European friends, but he was among the kindest men alive. Each weekend he would keep open house at his seaside home, giving away more in a day than some of his needier guests could earn in a week. For the daily grind of administration, by contrast, or for the harsh realities of political manœuvre, anyone less suitable would have been hard to find. Crisis followed crisis during his tenure of office but he was always perfect in one respect; as subject for the local cartoonist. Of the Singapore experts in this medium the best was one whose work was pervaded by irrelevant cats. In a typical cartoon David would appear as the conductor of an orchestra in which every other performer was equally David Marshall—with the one significant exception of Lee Kuan Yew. In the corner, however, one cat would be remarking to another—in casual reference to Han Suyin—that 'Love is a Many-Splendoured Thing.'

Other than for the cartoonist, however, David's premiership fell short of the ideal, nor was it ever clear how long it could last. I was made aware of crises by the Deputy Speaker asking me, from time to time, whether I could lend him a copy of Erskine May. At one crisis, however, I was actually present. Coming to see the Chief Minister by appointment, I found his office in a state of evident confusion. When the great man finally emerged from an inner room it was to apologise for having to cancel our talk. 'I have the whole cabinet in there,' he explained. 'We are just about to resign!' I forget whether he explained why but I tried, anyway, to talk him out of it. 'Look, David,' I urged, 'you mustn't do that!' 'But what else *can* we do?' he asked, and a brisk discussion followed. He finally remembered the cabinet and went back to them, having decided for the moment against resignation. Some twenty other people must have had a share in dissuading him and mine was probably negligible, but the incident reveals something of the atmosphere he created. His temperament was as unstable as his majority and the end was already in sight.

David Marshall fell from power while leading an all-party delegation to London, his object being to gain Singapore's independence in every respect and for purposes even of security and defence. The Secretary of State for the Colonies was the astute Mr Alan Lennox-Boyd, who perceived at once that there was no real agreement among the delegates themselves. From some motive which must remain obscure, he deftly broke the delegation up into its discordant elements and explained that so many divergent aims could not be reconciled. Still smarting from this experience, David was summoned to an interview with the Prime Minister, Sir Anthony Eden.

'On one point,' Eden began, 'I can set your mind at rest. You may have seen a newspaper story about Alan Lennox-Boyd being asked to resign. Well, there is no truth in it, none whatever, I couldn't possibly do without Alan. I feel, therefore, that I should assure you, first of all, that Alan is to stay.'

'But, but, but——!' spluttered David, who would have enjoyed the spectacle of Lennox-Boyd being boiled in oil.

'I realise,' Eden went on, 'that you have worked with Alan for some time and have got to know him. Any change at the Colonial Office would be undesirable in any case, but doubly so while your delegation is here. You will be glad to know that any immediate change is out of the question.'

'But, but, but——!' was David's only reply and the conversation continued on the same unpromising lines, Eden seeking to convince David that he need have no fear and that Lennox-Boyd would have the Colonial Office for ever, and David at a loss for words in which to express his loathing for that same indispensable statesman. Whether the discussion ever reached any more profitable theme I was not told but the parting words seem to have been the most interesting. As he rose to take his leave, David made some apology for his inexperience. As a new boy to politics he was a little overwhelmed, he said, to find himself opposed, at the outset, by one of Britain's greatest Foreign Ministers. It was a well-meant compliment but the result was somewhat unexpected. Looking away from him, and speaking quietly, Eden finished the sentence for him by adding: '. . . and its worst Prime Minister. . . .'

On this note the negotiations came to an end and the Singapore delegates returned severally to Singapore. David resigned at once but his place was taken by Lim Yew-Hock, who reached agreement (in 1957) with Eden's successor. There was to be no General Election in Singapore until 1959, but Lim Yew-Hock was already on the defensive against a party more extreme than his. The People's Action Party (P.A.P.) had only three candidates in 1955 but all three had been elected. It was rightly supposed, therefore, that the P.A.P. had wider support than their representation would suggest. But the disturbing fact about the P.A.P. was the extent of its Communist membership. In the existing state of civil war on the mainland, a mere adherence to the Malayan Communist Party was a punishable offence. To collect funds for the M.C.P. was more than that, a capital offence. So the party members had to enlist in some legally recognised party. Many were thus in the P.A.P. as the party of the furthest left. Some—and these the more dangerous— were outwardly Progressive. All, however, were Chinese and all could be assumed to favour Singapore's eventual annexation by China. But while the P.A.P. included these sinister elements, it also relied upon people whose socialism was at least compatible with citizenship. And the whole party was led by the enigmatic and forceful Lee Kuan Yew. Was he too a Communist? There was no certainty on this point. Were he as moderate, however, as some people professed to believe, the electoral success of the P.A.P. might be expected to end in his removal from the party leadership. There is scarcely an example of anyone's success in riding

LEE KUAN YEW

that particular tiger. The moderate leader of a partly Communist party may expect to die before long in a motoring accident. No experienced commentator would expect to find him still in power after five years of independence. That is nevertheless what the historian will have to record. Lee Kuan Yew won a landslide victory in 1959 and is still in office today.

The surname Lee is one of the very few which can be either Chinese or English. My wife thus edited the agony column in the Malayan *Sunday Times* under the name of Jane Lee. Seekers of advice could suppose her to be a Christian Chinese, an expatriate Englishwoman, an American descendant of the Confederate General, or even (for that matter) a Singapore-born Eurasian; for each of these possibilities would have been at least consistent with the 'Casebook' heading. There was nothing unusual therefore in the future Prime Minister being christened Harry Lee by his methodist parents. But the westernised name was but the beginning of what was to be a westernised career. From an English school he went on to read Law at Cambridge. Graduating with distinction, he was then called to the Bar and so returned to practise in Singapore where he married a woman whose education had been very similar. When I first met him he was still called Harry, being also a pipe-smoker and well known on the local golf-course. Although purely Chinese in descent and appearance, he might have seemed to be English by choice. He certainly knew no Chinese at that time, English being the language of his education, his profession and the society in which he moved. His background should have made him a typical Progressive but that was a party in which other and older Chinese were already dominant. They would never have accepted so young a man as leader, and it was only as leader that he would consent to serve. The P.A.P., however, the party of the minor trades unions, was itself a very young group and almost without professional ability of any kind. Harry Lee brought them the answer to many of their problems, taking the chair as a matter of course. In the first elected Legislature it was not the defeated Progressives that David Marshall had to worry about. He stood face to face, rather, with Harry Lee.

On becoming Prime Minister, Harry Lee became Lee Kuan Yew. It was rumoured that he was learning Chinese and suspected that he had been Communist all along. But Harry Lee was not Communist. His policy was to be as far to the left as possible, short of communism, and further to the left in words than in action. But where was he to draw the line? Whatever the term may mean in other parts of the world, the Singapore Communist is one who seeks to incorporate Singapore (with Malaysia) into the Nanyang Province of China. By this definition Lee Kuan Yew has never been a Communist. His aim has been to associate Singapore more closely with Malaysia and then maintain Malaysian independence against all comers; with himself no doubt as the chosen leader. In the meanwhile he realises that Singapore, like Hongkong, owes everything to its international trade, with its port open to all the world, with its developing industries still subsidiary, Singapore would die at once under the Chinese flag. Religious and political intolerance is something the Singaporeans can never afford. They must remain on good terms with their customers, whoever they may be, and any other policy would be suicidal. Of all this Lee Kuan Yew is fully aware, and his apparently impossible task has been to satisfy the extremists in his party without killing the trade upon which their livelihood (and his) must depend. This is the task that he has managed to perform, and astonished observers are bound to wonder how. What sort of a man have the Singaporeans accepted as their leader?

Lee Kuan Yew is of medium height and build, bullet-headed and narrow-eyed, obviously intellectual and resolute. Utterly without charm, his expression is one of barely-concealed contempt; for his opponents, for his followers, perhaps for himself. He works far harder than his colonialist

Lee Kuan Yew

predecessors, and now speaks not only English and Chinese but Malay and some Tamil as well. He has had his close associates from the beginning but one cannot imagine that they are his friends or that he is even capable of friendship. He makes no effort to conciliate or cajole. While Singapore was still under 'colonial' rule, and he closely watched by the police, he would dine with Europeans but without softening his air of contemptuous hostility.

In those days my wife and I used to invite our History Honours students to hold a fortnightly meeting at our house. One of them would read a paper, often on a political theme, and a discussion would follow, ending with drinks and an informal party. If there was a distinguished guest, he would dine with us first, and I remember one boy's dismay when he realised that his paper would be read to the Chief Minister as well as to his classmates. But David Marshall presented no real problem, being ready to applaud and still more eager to do the talking himself. Lee Kuan Yew presented a complete contrast in manner. The students, remember, were the future civil servants and journalists, the embryo politicians and teachers, the very people a party leader should seek to influence. One would have expected to see the attempt being made, with interest and flattery used as prelude to a display of statesmanship. But Lee Kuan Yew listened in grim silence, said nothing in compliment and seemed reluctant to say anything at all. When he eventually voiced an opinion, it was more with the object of exposing folly than of revealing wisdom. He despised his audience and left them, finally, more disheartened than impressed. Or had he made an impression which I was unable to appreciate? As compared with the mass of the P.A.P. voters, these university students, whether Chinese, Malay, Indian or Eurasian, were of course highly westernised. Their response could not have been typical of the population at large. But I doubt whether the supremely introvert Lee Kuan Yew adjusted his manner to this or to any other group. All that he gave out (whether intentionally or not) was a sense of intellectual superiority, an utter contempt for any opposition, and a basic detachment from the world of poverty, emotion and youth. This is the impression he still makes on television viewers. If not himself a Communist, Lee Kuan Yew has at least the Communist's gift for inspiring fear. And he had the air, from the start, of one who regards his own success as a certainty.

We shall never know the full story of Lee Kuan Yew's rise to power nor of his subsequent battle to retain it. The historian never learns the full story about anything; nor, if he did, would there be time to tell it or a public that would believe. We can safely conclude, however, that one clue to his achievement lies in his ability to play one opponent against another. Singapore politics involve a complex pattern of overlapping pressure groups, racial, religious, linguistic, economic, military and criminal. Lee Kuan Yew has induced the British to imprison his more disloyal supporters, publicly protesting against this violation of the rights of man. He has used the Federation of Malaya to counterbalance the Singapore trades unions. He has used the mob to intimidate the merchants and the merchants to influence the Colonial Office. He illustrates perpetually the principle that it is better to have two enemies than one. But there is more to his career than that and one factor in it is clearly the balance he exemplifies between what is western and what is oriental. As seen from London he may pass as purely Chinese, inscrutable, secretive, ruthless, dogmatic and superior. As seen from Peking he may look more like a golf-playing British barrister. And either description is correct. Like many people in Singapore he is heir to several cultures of unusual complexity, the blend finally achieved being largely a matter of choice. Such has been the interaction of East and West that the 'purely' western or 'purely' oriental is non-existent. As between these hypothetical opposites, however, there are many sorts of compromise. One has to live in a place like Singapore to realise that racial origin is far less important, in this context, than personal preference. We are, within limits, what we choose to be.

Lee Kuan Yew is unique in the success of his political career but a typical Singaporean in his blend of attitudes. And for me, while in the East, the most absorbing problem was always to discover when, why and how the great civilisations had come to differ. The eventual result was the book, *East and West*, in which I tried to explain the conclusions I had reached. But I felt, while making this attempt, that the book should have been written by a Singapore Eurasian or by a Europeanised Asian, by someone for whom the contrast and conflict was ever present in the mind. My colleagues, friends and pupils included Chinese so westernised as to be hardly distinguishable from the British, people of such complex origin as Jewish Armenians or Portuguese Malays, British too Malayanised to live outside Malaya, and people whose outlook seemed to fluctuate as readily as their dress. Some day one of these should tell us what we need to know about our own civilisation and its opposite. There is reason to suppose, however, that the needed book will not appear tomorrow. For those in the best position to explain the situation seem often to display not a cultural blend but a split personality. A very learned Bishop once sought to discover what value there may be in Chinese medicine. Singling out an intelligent young man from among the initiated Chinese practitioners, he sent him to qualify in European medicine, hoping that he would then be able to compare the two systems as one with a knowledge of both. Although successful in all his examinations, the subject of this experiment could explain nothing. His mind had become compartmented to the point at which he could say, 'The Chinese treatment would be this, the European treatment would be that,' without being able to give any opinion as to which treatment might be the more likely to succeed. Nor has the opposite process produced a very much better result. The Englishman who really masters the Chinese language, intending subsequently to explain (say) Chinese political thought, must usually become a philologist in the process, having no interest finally in anything but language. The obstacles to any mutual understanding lie thus not merely between minds but between different areas of the same personality.

Whatever the difficulties may be, a city like Singapore has the intellectual opportunities which were once used to the full in Damascus, Alexandria, Byzantium and Venice. What it cannot afford, in making the most of its position, is the emotion of hatred. Is Lee Kuan Yew as free of it as could be wished? Was the P.A.P. attack on the University a rational policy or the result of ignorance and prejudice? In one human quality, at least, he would seem to be sadly deficient and that is in his sense of humour. He can jeer at a fallen opponent or pour scorn on a ridiculous proposal. That he can otherwise take pleasure in the merely funny has still perhaps to be proved. It is in this sense, more especially, that he may seem more sinister than he is. For there is no more dreadful sight than the elderly face of the Communist schoolboy; that wooden, concentrated and expressionless look, of which Lee Kuan Yew has more than a trace. It is the imprint of the Chinese Middle and High Schools, the visible sign of an intellectual castration. Lee Kuan Yew would be further from this image if he could laugh more readily and more kindly at all that is absurd. Or does he fear that laughter bears the stigma of Malaya's colonialist past? When the British recovered Singapore from the Japanese, their first move (the story goes) was to level the cricket pitch, their second to plan a race meeting. This legend, true or false, is no proof in itself of intelligence, but could indicate a sense of humour that present Singaporeans might do well to copy. Some other people in the same situation would have planned a massacre.

Is it feasible to form a self-governing multi-racial society? Given a mixture of black and white, it is obviously impossible. With a blend of brown and yellow there would seem to be more chance of success, shortlived as the Malaysian experiment has actually proved. After all, the different racial and religious groups could live happily together under British rule. Can they submit as readily, however, to their own government? This remains to be seen. But what may or may not be possible for the adult population is certainly feasible for the children. In the schools where English has been taught the pupils seem to possess an additional fund of tolerance and gaiety. My university students could be rebellious as against authority but I recall no instance of their offending each other in matters of religion or race. In many or most respects their politeness was exemplary. As for the misunderstandings which must arise in their society from linguistic error, these formed the basis of their humour. There is hope for Singapore in the charming manners which these children display. On at least one occasion, moreover, they enacted a scene in which the lesson was made plain for all to see. It was in the concluding scene of the Historical Pageant of 1956, when the stage gradually filled with High School pupils each in a different type of costume—cheongsum, sarong or sari—and exemplifying a different racial group. After each one had appeared, with a word of commentary, they all joined hands in a big circle and began a dance to slow music. As the curtain fell for the last time the circle was revolving, unbroken, as a symbol of the friendship which can exist between people whose customs differ but whose gentleness is the same. Beyond a certain point this closing scene represented more of an aspiration than a fact, but it related also to something that has been accomplished, the daily miracle of the Singapore streets, the way in which people live together. What has been so nearly achieved could be a good omen for the future. More than that, it could be an example to the world.

10

RICHARD MIERS

The night before the battle we started the evening in the officers' mess of the South Wales Borderers, moved to a cocktail party given by the Malay Regiment, and ended where we had begun over brandy and cigars. Back in Singapore our wives (Richard's and mine) were shuddering to think what hardships we might be undergoing in the jungle. We were, in point of fact, discussing literature, grand opera, psychology and art. Those present, about six in all, included Evan Davies of the Special Branch whose Machiavellian schemes added such colour to the local conflict. Richard took this opportunity to tell the story of Evan's most dramatic arrest. Hiding near the track junction at midnight, he and Evan had finally heard the stealthy sound of their victim's approach. The Communist master mind was about to fall into the trap. Evan leapt at his prey and snapped on the handcuffs with one swift and practised motion. They fell off again, however, sliding from the twig-like wrists of a Chinese girl aged about fourteen. She was the agent all right but of lesser calibre than they had been led to hope. The master mind (if there was one) had escaped again.

It was an amusing evening and Richard was in wonderful form. As the C.O. of the 1st Battalion, South Wales Borderers, he had already made a name for himself as the army's expert in jungle warfare; as the author, indeed, of the official textbook. He had earned the D.S.O. in World War II, at the end of which he had been commanding a battalion. A big man of tremendous vitality, a born soldier and idolised by his men, he tackled each phase of his active career with the gusto of one who found it all terrific fun. Able to think as well as act, full of ideas and having a natural eloquence, Richard was bound to rise (as we all agreed) to the highest rank. In extracting the last ounce of effort from his troops, Richard applied a powerful mixture of ruthlessness and charm. For other units the war was merely a job. For Richard's men it was a crusade, to be epitomised later in the title of his book *Shoot to Kill*. We were brought together through Richard's attractive and scholarly wife, Sue, who had joined the University as a Lecturer in my department. Richard and Sue were among our dearest friends, as Sue is still, and it was this relationship which had brought me (as war correspondent) to the fringes of the war. With me had come Scotty Royce, the American historian who was temporarily Sue's colleague and mine. The most stimulating sort of conversation continued for much of the night but at three or thereabouts we finally went to bed. After all, Richard reminded us, there was a war on, and we should be ready to go at five.

In the hour or so before daybreak things happened very quickly. Dressing in jungle green and grabbing our borrowed carbines, we tore off in a jeep to the airstrip from which the helicopters were to operate. The roads were alive with trucks and lorries, scout cars and motor-cycles. An area of jungle was to be cordoned off by police while a Brigade moved through it, and one Company of infantry dropped into the centre. It was this Company that we now saw removed by helicopter, six men at a time, the machines running a sort of ferry service to the dropping zone and back. When the day had fairly begun we joined one of the columns in its move to the jungle's fringe; a column led, as it happened, by the present Lord Chalfont (Minister for—of all things—Disarmament) who was then merely Major Gwynne-Jones. Platoons moved off swiftly and there was little more to do than wait. We waited, however, in vain. No contact with the enemy was made. There was no enemy there, nor perhaps had there ever been. What was depressing, however, was not the lack of result—which would not be certain until days had passed—but the speed with which whole formations could be swallowed up by the landscape. To search a single hill feature properly, to be certain that there was nobody there, would have required not a Brigade but a Division. There was no Division, of course, available, nor could it have been maintained in the jungle had it been ordered into it. Faced by those tree-covered hills one came to realise that the need was not for armies but for information. Given the position of an enemy camp, one could do something about it. But without a six-figure map reference the hunt was hopeless. All depended finally on the relationship established between men like Evan Davies and men like Richard Miers. Theirs, as it happened, was a partnership which worked very well indeed. It could result, as it eventually did, in the sort of success which eliminated Goh Peng Tuan's gang. That operation revealed something of Richard's potential greatness as a soldier. Having pinpointed an enemy camp, temporarily vacant, and having ascertained—from Evan—the date by which it would again be occupied, Richard had every motive for attempting to surround the area. His Battalion's local prestige depended, after all, on the number of their eliminated opponents. But Richard decided, against much expert advice, that the solution, in this case, was an air strike. The result was a brilliant victory, in the terms of this particular conflict, but an addition to the score of the R.A.F. With this sort of achievement behind him, Richard was already becoming a legend.

What sort of man was he? What lay behind the growing legend? I have described him as a born soldier and this is perhaps the first point to underline. He came of a military family, long associated with Brecon and the Welsh countryside from which his men were drawn. 'As a boy,' says his younger brother, 'and as a young man, he was intelligent, sensitive and tremendously generous—determined and brave in the face of all sorts of adversity.' His must have been an unhappy childhood, for 'He was frankly disliked by my mother and wholly misunderstood by my father.' Both his strength and weakness might have thus the same origin, as his brother suggests: 'I think the result of the combination was a strong desire to prove himself in his work and in his friendships—and a necessity for confirmation of approval and affection. It always seemed to me that this was his driving force and that a more normal upbringing might have made him a less brilliant soldier.' There had never been any question in his mind as to what his profession should be. The line of his progress from Cheltenham to Sandhurst, from the South Wales Borderers to the Staff College, had all been plotted before he was born. He learnt to ride in the hunting field, learnt to shoot in the autumn woods. No one was ever to question his courage or loyalty; nor, for that matter, his ability and gift for leadership. Much of this was plainly inherited and as much again derived from the family environment. Brecon he loved as 'one of the most lovely and unspoilt places left in the United Kingdom'. From this background he derived the first quality essential to military leadership; a serene belief in himself. He was to worry in later years over his chances of promotion but he can never have questioned his own right to a command of some sort. An officer drawn from the ranks may become fussily authoritative in trying to overcome some basic insecurity. He can avoid this, sometimes, through being sufficiently tall. But Richard had that advantage too. Up to a certain point his success must have seemed inevitable.

To a reputation for gallantry Richard added a reputation for brains. There are civilians who think that the soldier is stupid, which is false. What is true, however, is that the soldier must not be too clever in an academic way. The too ingenious plan, like the too ingenious weapon, breaks down on the field of battle. The originality that can be of value must be modified by a robust common sense. It must be applied with a realisation of what is likely to go wrong. The soldier's instinctive rejection of the unworkably clever idea gains him, sometimes, the reputation for an absurd sort of conservatism. By the end of a long period without active service this reputation can even be deserved. In time of war, however, and during the aftermath, when senior officers have recent war experience, the soldier has all the cleverness that he can safely apply. Richard could be as original as anyone in conversation but he stopped short of making originality an end in itself. His aim was to kill terrorists, not to show how cleverly it could be done. When he left Malaya it was on promotion. He commanded a Brigade in Kenya and went from there to the Imperial Defence College. Success in one further post would have made him a Major-General but that was a rank he was never to reach.

So far there might be nothing in my description which might not apply to a score of other senior officers. But Richard, true to form in his professional career, had wider interests than most men of his type. Instead of marrying the daughter of some Welsh squire—or the daughter, for that matter, of an Adjutant-General—he fell in love with an American student of colonial history; one who taught, moreover, at the University of London. Apart from being born in the Belgian Congo, Sue's background is Maryland— where her mother is a painter of note. And so far from accepting meekly the position of Colonel's wife, Sue has always continued to be an active scholar and teacher. This never made her neglect the welfare of the troops but it made her complementary rather than merely ancillary to Richard. She had always, as she still has, a career of her own and indeed a nationality of her own. They differed almost dramatically in size, Sue being as short as Richard was tall. It was this problem which my Ann had presented to her in her agony column capacity. The letter came apparently from the short wife of a tall husband, and told of the difficulty which prevented their walking together, his normal pace being the equivalent of her speed in running. What were they to do? Ann guessed that the letter was from

Richard but answered it, nevertheless, in her capacity as Jane Lee. 'Ride bicycles,' was Ann's advice; not necessarily of much value to those whose road movements needed to be covered, normally, by an armoured escort. Richard was an exceptional man and not least so in his marriage. For long childless, they eventually had a family, with young Charles as a possible successor in the Regiment. There may be other soldiers yet with the name of Miers.

Looking back on their years together, Sue remembers, first of all, Richard's tremendous vitality and gusto:

> The general impression made was one of immense vigour and personality—someone who came in and tossed the children in the air. He was terribly funny in small ways. He would drive into a village and solemnly shout 'Which way?' at anyone standing around, just to see if they would say, 'Straight on!'—just as he sometimes waved at a complete stranger to get a reaction. Once on a Nile ferry boat he doubled up with mirth when a fisherman offered a fish for a shilling. When he had the whole boat laughing and the price reduced to fourpence he confided to me that the shilling price seemed very reasonable. When we lived in a four-roomed house with a garden the size of a pocket handkerchief, he said to his father after lunch, 'Care to see the place?' and took him out of the front door and a minute later in at the back. On another occasion his father revoked when partnering Richard at bridge. Richard said nothing but revoked later against his father.

Richard had a great interest in anyone who could be regarded as a 'character'. His father headed the list of such personalities, figuring in some of the best of his stories. He told me once of a pool near his home which was over-shadowed by a high crag. He and his brother dared each other to dive from it. Overhearing these taunts their father came out with a plank and fixed it half-way up an over-hanging tree, thus adding another six or ten feet to a height already fearsome enough. Saying nothing at all, he returned presently in a striped Victorian bathing costume, dived from the plank, went home and never came near the place again. It was some time before Richard or his brother dared imitate the feat, which illustrates one aspect at least of his peculiar upbringing.

It was a Polish officer who once told G. K. Chesterton that there are two possible careers for a man of spirit; that of cavalryman and that of poet. Were these alternatives widened so as to include all soldiers and all authors, the aphorism might meet with a fairly general acceptance. We should feel sympathy at least with the point of view. And such an amateur soldier as I have been could find comfort in having done with the pen what I had failed to do with the sword. But Richard, with his D.S.O. and Bar, had no reason to fear comparisons even as an author. It is the sad fact that he could write more effectively than most of the present folk whose works pass as literature. Take as example this account of the bombing strike against the Goh Peng Tuan gang:

> Now we could hear them. A steady drone of engines getting nearer and, looking behind us, we could see in the sky, perhaps ten miles away, a cluster of tiny specks flying steadily towards us, like a skein of wild geese. On they came, ominous and inexorable, to thunder over our heads and to pass on towards the target.
>
> 'Fifteen seconds to go.'
>
> We were all on our feet now, leaning forward, eyes glued on the target.
>
> 'Counting down now,' came Mike's voice, flatly unemotional. 'Five—Four—Three—Two—One. BOMBS AWAY.'
>
> We went on looking towards the target. The aircraft flew serenely on. Reason told us that it was too far away to see the falling bombs, but during the next few seconds we had time to wonder whether, like a damp squib at a children's party, there had been some hitch. But all at once a great rectangular rent opened in the backcloth of

jungle, the ground trembled under our feet, and through my field-glasses I could see in the cloud of dust and rubble, broken lengths of tree being tossed into the air as though they were matchsticks.

This was not the end of the show. There was more to come. Buzzing over the target like a mosquito the Auster aircraft now dropped its marker balloons. Then screeching over our heads with the wrath of God came two squadrons of silvery sleek Canberra jet bombers, to wheel on to the target and stoke the dust cloud to even bigger proportions. Their tremendous speed made marker balloons necessary as a safety precaution.

At last it was over and the aircraft, wearing it almost seemed, a look of relief and smug satisfaction, departed on their way.

'A bit of a sledgehammer to crack a nut,' said Evan who would, one felt, have preferred more subtle methods . . . 'But worth it if we've hit them.'

(Shoot to Kill. Faber, London, 1959, pp. 68–9)

They had been hit all right, although heaven knows how the bomb-aimers had done it. From a helicopter afterwards the jungle round there looked all alike to me. To identify that target in a split second, with no more clue than the edge of a practically invisible swamp, still seems to me an extraordinary feat. The point of the quotation, however, is the author's style. For its purpose it could not be bettered. Phrases like 'ominous and inexorable', 'with the wrath of God', 'silvery sleek' and 'smug satisfaction' linger afterwards in the memory. Richard could certainly describe any scene he had witnessed. He was expert, too, in conveying the humour of it, as witness the last page of *Shoot to Kill.* In it he refers to the surrender of Public Enemy No. 1 in the Segamat area:

And what happened to Ming Lee? If we British find it difficult to understand the mentality of the C.T. [Communist-Terrorists], it is a fair bet that they find it equally difficult to understand us. Ming Lee, that former

153

terror of the neighbourhood, spent a brief sojourn in the Government Rehabilitation Centre. After which, as a free man, he returned to Segamat, where he is now employed as groundsman to the local cricket club.

And they say the pitch at Segamat has never been in better condition.

(Ibid., p. 213)

After our Malayan days were over, Richard and I next came together in the United States. This was in October 1958 and the meeting took place when a lecturing engagement brought me to Washington, D.C. As Sue and Richard were staying with Sue's mother at Bethesda we were able to spend some time together, and we seized the opportunity to visit the battlefield of Gettysburg. We glimpsed Eisenhower's helicopter while on the way there and were told that he was not the friendly local squire except at election times. Then we found ourselves on the most self-conscious battlefront in the world, littered with obelisks and cannon, a monument to mark the position of every Brigade, a plaque to show where every field officer had been killed in action. It is tremendously impressive in a way but the efforts made are all commemorative rather than explanatory. A study of the model and the map, the guidebook and the ground leave one with only a vague impression of what either General was trying to do. And why call it 'Pickett's Charge' when it was an infantry assault? After we had finished our pacing of the stricken field we came to the conclusion that neither side, on that day, had been particularly bright. 'It looks to me,' said Richard, 'as if Lee and Meade must have been equally below their usual form.' With that verdict I was inclined to agree, but I went on to be critical about something else. In Washington they have the theatre where President Lincoln was assassinated, afterwards turned into offices but now on view to the public. Why, for heaven's sake, don't they restore the theatre to its original use and in its original form? Why don't they perform, each year, the play which the President had come to

RICHARD MIERS

see? It would do more for Lincoln's memory than his
monument can do, and would have the further merit of
emphasising the fact that the U.S.A. once had a President
who went to the theatre. It was admittedly to happen
again, but he too was murdered. The more cultured Pre-
sidents do not seem, in fact, to be the most fortunate.
By the time Richard had finished his tour of duty in
Kenya, Ann and I had established ourselves in Guernsey.
There the Miers family joined us in the autumn of 1961. We
all had a splendid holiday together, taking occasion to visit
both Alderney and Sark. Richard and I made a brief survey
of the German fortifications in each island. They reminded
us both of the British efforts to fortify Singapore. The
oddest feature of the Singapore forts is the legend attached
to them; that their guns would not bear on the side from
which the Japanese actually attacked. This story, to which
Churchill himself has given currency, would be impressive if
it were only true. Most of the guns had, in fact, a 360
degree traverse; the exception being those originally mounted
in a battleship, which retained the dead arc of their naval
mounting—the arc representing the ship's own super-
structure. Not only would they bear but some of them were
in action for two days, firing until the gunners were exhausted and their ammunition spent. Whoever was responsible for the fall of Singapore, it was not the officer who
sited its fixed defences nor even the officer who allocated
them (sensibly enough) a high proportion of armour-piercing
shell. But the fortifications in Alderney and Guernsey tell a
different story, never having been in action. On the British
forts—in which no enemy had shown an interest—were
superimposed the German emplacements; which no one
ever attacked. However costly they had been to construct
and maintain, the works had been tamely surrendered and
as tamely handed back. It seemed doubtful to me whether
these pillboxes could have served any purpose at the best of
times. For one thing, they were sited, some of them, to
cover stretches of coastline where only a lunatic would

dream of landing. Those which enfilade the more promising beaches have an arc, in some instances, which excludes their own frontage; a doubtful practice, at best. But behind all the questions of detail there loomed another question of policy, for the British cannot have wanted the Channel Islands in the first instance. Had they been tactically important, they could hardly have been given up. If they were not important, why should there be any special plan for their recapture? All these questions Richard was happy to brush aside. He could not see the fortifications as much more than a joke. Their sole purpose, to him, was manifest. They were meant to impress the inspecting General.

A year or two later I met one of the German generals, Count von Schmettow. It was at a cocktail party in Guernsey and I longed to ask him whether Richard's surmise was correct. Would a German general be candid about this, even in peacetime, even after retirement? My knowledge of German is scanty, however, and his knowledge of English seemed hardly more fluent. So I merely asked him whether he enjoyed revisiting Guernsey and was glad to be told that he was enjoying it immensely.

Richard and Sue lived at Camberley while he attended his course at the I.D.C. and it was there that we all met again. Each day Richard went up to London wearing a dark suit and bowler hat, carrying a briefcase and umbrella. Other men, identically dressed and as unmistakably Aldershot, would greet each other and him on the platform. On one such trip, he told me about his course, which involved some fieldwork. He and another officer, about as senior, were sent to broaden their minds by a visit to the I.B.M. stand at Olympia or Earl's Court. They were cordially received by an executive who had no idea of what organisation they were supposed to represent. Showing them the different types of computer and explaining their respective merits, their guide fished patiently for information about their business. Perceiving this, Richard decided to save him from disappointment. He confessed to being Managing-

Richard Miers

Director of a pretty big concern, engaged upon unspecified work of more than national importance. He hinted that the smaller computers on display were no better than those his firm had already in use. Clutching at this small piece of information, the I.B.M. man asked for details—what equipment did they use and for what purpose? Waving his cigar with an expansive gesture, Richard professed an all but complete ignorance of the merely technical side of his company's affairs. 'I don't profess to know all the details,' he admitted disarmingly, 'So I was careful to bring my Works Manager with me.' (He indicated his fellow student from the I.D.C.) 'Mr Willis here can give you all the information you want. He has been with the firm for twenty-five years—or is it twenty-seven?—and knows the whole business from A to Z. So do tell this gentleman, Willis, about the computers we have had in use since 1959. One of them has been a disappointment, I know, but I can't recall either its make or its purpose. Your big chance, Willis, has come. The floor is yours!' What the Air-Commodore made of this assignment I was never told. But the I.D.C. certainly included men who could have coped with the situation, Major-General Frank Brooke being one of them. It was he, I think, who introduced me there to Wing-Commander Foxley-Norris. The name reminded me of my childhood at York and I said at once, 'You must be the son, surely, of Dean Foxley-Norris?' I was shattered by his response. 'The Dean of York? No, that was my grandfather.' I realised that old age was creeping on; that it had, in fact, arrived. It was Richard who did something to restore my morale. We were crossing the Horse Guards Parade and entered the archway leading into Whitehall. The lifeguardsman on duty saluted and I observed to Richard that he was obviously a Brigadier, even in civilian clothes. 'Oh?' he replied innocently, 'I thought that salute was for you!' We never met again.

In the process by which men rise to eminence in their calling they are faced by successive obstacles, the first of them at school. There follow successive tests of character and courage, more riders being eliminated at every fence. The jumps are higher as the winning-post comes in sight but those still in the running have the confidence which results from all that they have so far achieved. Among the last and biggest of the obstacles is the temptation to give up the race, play for safety and take one's ease. Tired, and shaken by the last fence (which we only just cleared, touch and go), we feel that we have done enough. For Richard that temptation came with the offer of a civilian career, one that would have given him an honourable status in the county that he loved. He wavered, as we all do, and then turned the offer down. He had reached that late stage in a man's career when he can look around and count the riders left in a rapidly thinning field. But there was one fence left, the one we tend to forget, and that was where Richard's career came to its abrupt end.

At the time of his tragic death, Richard, who was often mentioned as a future C.I.G.S., held an appointment in Germany which would have made him a Major-General. He might have gone on to command a Division but fate decreed otherwise. He came down at the last fence of all, eliminated by the sort of accident which could happen to almost anyone. As each year passes and as British troops become involved in places like Borneo, there are those still in command who will think, 'This is where we need a man like Richard Miers.' But among his friends as opposed to his fellow-leaders the same thought will take a different form: 'How Richard would have loved to meet this absurd person!' or simply, 'How Richard would have laughed at that!' Gifted in every way, brilliant and resolute in action, entertaining as a companion and loyal as a friend, Richard was among the finest men of his generation. Shall we, I wonder, breed such men again?

11

***

SIBYL HATHAWAY

We first discovered the Channel Islands in 1956, led there by the need to interview a retired rubber planter called Harry Piper. I was immersed at that time in studying the early history of the rubber industry, an important phase in the development of what is now called Malaysia. On leave from Singapore, we stayed with the legendary Mr Piper in September, saw something of Jersey, and went on to visit Guernsey, Sark, Herm and Alderney. It was all too brief and we were back in Singapore by 2 October. We were not then thinking of an early withdrawal from the academic world but it did occur to us that the Channel Islands might provide a suitable home whenever the time for retirement should come. Children born in the East soon reach the age at which any further stay in the tropics would be educationally disastrous; and where they go, the parents must eventually follow. While it is true, then, that we were studying the Channel Islands with interest in 1956, we had decided nothing at that time and I, at least, retained some affection for the Isle of Man, in which I had been stationed at one time during the war. I even owned some property there, an old mill which I had planned to convert and develop. Of the Channel Islands, however, our first preference was for Alderney; an island which seemed to have great, if unrealised, possibilities.

It will be seen that my wife and I have a definite interest in islands. Singapore is one and Penang, where we spent a belated honeymoon, is another. We were later to show interest in Vancouver Island, and my wife had to restrain me from purchasing the lease of Lihou. What is so attractive about an island? It offers, first of all, a finite problem. Whether it is to be explored, studied, administered or developed, the task seems inherently feasible. Nothing stretches on indefinitely, there is no horizon to be chased, no problem hopelessly linked with another more distant, no blurred edges and doubtful fringe. Whether considered geographically, historically, agriculturally or socially, an island situation begins and ends at the water's edge. Assuming, moreover, that the island is of no great size, it allows scope for the individual. We need not discuss the needs and aspirations of people in the abstract—classes and masses, proletariat and meritocracy—for the folk we are concerned with are known to us by name. These are the more rational grounds for choosing the island life. They are not (I suspect) the real ones. For an island is essentially a toy, a society in miniature, a replica on a reduced scale of something which exists in real life. It attracts in much the same way as a model railway or village, appealing to the more boyish side of our characters. Within the limits of an island one can play the part of monarch, seaman or statesman, engineer, architect, or farmer. For those especially with a number of interests and with varying moods, an island is the most fascinating toy in the world. We may want to escape from it periodically so as to regain our sense of proportion, but we return with the greater sense of homecoming and peace.

The mere mention of the word 'escape' must suggest a further element in the island lover's personality. If he needs to escape from his island, is not the island itself a means of escape from the world? There is one sense in which this suggestion would be, for me, the reverse of the truth. From an island one can view the problems of the world with a certain detachment, making up in sanity for what one may lack in urgency or fire. But in another sense, escape was, for me, essential, for while I could live in the intellectual atmosphere of the modern city—in New York, San Francisco or even (with more reluctance) in London—I could not endure the traffic. My mental processes are geared, like my powers of observation, to the pace of the dog-cart, rowing boat or bicycle. I take no pleasure in rapid transit, whether by land, sea or air. I feel, moreover, that speed means noise and that noise means mental paralysis. So far from being able to think in an airliner, I can scarcely pretend to do anything significant within earshot of a busy highway. For me, and for many other people, the modern world is becoming impossible, not because of frayed nerves but because of inability to work against a background of traffic. We can seek to remedy the situation by explaining how the city of the future should be planned, but this does nothing for the city of the present. Nor have we the peace and quiet in which to outline the project for recovering quiet and peace. So the immediate remedy lies in escape to an island where life moves more slowly, where the noise at night is of the wind in the treetops or the surf on the beach; to an island where people still matter more than vehicles.

The central and immediate problem of the modern world concerns the automobile. We may be concerned, and rightly, about over-population. We may feel apprehensive about the application of nuclear physics to foreign policy. We may foresee future conflicts between East and West; as also, for that matter, between Black and White. But the motor-car is already laying our society waste, being far more dangerous than the aircraft, far more lethal than the Bomb. The car would be a splendid vehicle if nobody else possessed one. Once made common to all it changes our way of life dramatically and for the worse. Nor are traffic accidents more than incidental to the problem we have to face. They are admittedly comparable to the casualties incurred in many a past campaign. They far exceed those reported after some of the most decisive battles. But the damage done by cars which collide is as nothing compared with the harm done by those which speed on; by those, for that matter, which merely park. So little are we aware of this menace that our misgivings have scarcely been defined and our plans for survival have not even been formulated. Saying little, we have done nothing.

First step in the disastrous process is the flight from the city. So far as our industrial cities are concerned we began to desert them, admittedly, before the motor-car was invented. It is the car, nevertheless, which has hastened the process and created the suburbs to which people have largly withdrawn. As the city loses its magnetism, particularly after dark, its cultural life declines. People who have fled to the suburbs at nightfall are reluctant to return for the concert or theatre. They make a new suburban life for themselves, centred on the garage, the garden and the television set. Cities less industrialised may remain attractive, but less to their traditional residents than to the visitor, the foreigner, the negro and the poor. For the country's effectively active population there is created the life of the supermarket, the commuter station, the quiet sidestreet and the plate-glass school. The children are relatively safe from the traffic and the nights are relatively free from the noise. By the standards of the last century the suburban life is almost incredibly comfortable and affluent. In all essentials a middle-class Utopia would seem to have been achieved with each small family turned in on itself, away from the public house and away from the neighbours, with do-it-yourself carpentry for the husband, television for the children, and hire-purchased luxury for the wife.

A suburban population should be, in theory, completely content. After all, what more can they want? In point of fact, people are dissatisfied and restless. Far from being content with the suburb, they feel vaguely cheated. Theirs is a sense of loss which they cannot themselves explain. Without realising it, they miss the city and the country. It was to the city that two previous generations had looked for inspiration. The city had offered excitement and stimulus, with political meetings and occasional riot, with murder trials and state occasions, the gossip of the market and the talk of the town. Earlier generations had looked for inspiration to the countryside and the village. Of this the memory is more remote but it remains the background for the fairy story, the legend of romance, the more nostalgic of our novels and films. The suburban garden is a model of the country we have never known, the shopping-centre a poor substitute for the city we have mislaid. But people reveal their discontent more in what they do than in what they say. Far from being happy in the suburb, they see the motor-car as their means of escape. On each holiday and on each fine weekend they go in search of something they have lost.

There is a sense in which people go to seek a world which never existed. In a far more real sense the world they want is there until the moment of their arrival. The traveller from the suburb wants to visit a real city, a place which centres upon its cathedral or castle, a place of narrow streets where the church bells sound the hour, where stalls clutter the market place and where the Judge can be glimpsed on his way to the Assizes. A real city has a character of its own and a sense of civic pride. Whether it is York or Salisbury, Canterbury or Winchester, it defies imitation and claims respect. Here is a place, one feels, where things have happened and where things may happen again. A proclamation might be read from the City Hall, the garrison might be called to arms, a tyrant might be denounced from the pulpit or a King received at the City Gates. Here is the spot where a duel was fought and this is the Inn where Dickens stayed. Were we to live here we should be within an easy walk of the Theatre, the Library, the Assembly Rooms and the High Street. All this we have lost or have never had, our homes not being even in Liverpool but in Wallasey; not even in London but at Golders Green. All we can do, to console ourselves, is to drive on the occasional weekend to the cities that are nearest, to Gloucester or Chester, to Beverley or Bath. Tired in the evening, we find ourselves back in Solihull or Bootle, Cheadle Hulme or Penge.

The older urge is towards the country. Here the dream takes in the silence of the hills and noises of the farmyard. Away from the roar of traffic, we shall hear only the ripple of the streams and the song of the thrush. Later in the day we shall visit the old inn, where we saw the hounds meet on Boxing Day. Almost opposite are the gates of the Manor House, beyond which again we can glimpse the Rectory elms. Part Tudor, part Georgian, the village street winds along the river bank. Opposite stand the Abbey ruins and behind them the farm buildings where Oliver Cromwell is said to have stabled his horses. This is the countryside of our ancestors, the world of the Miller and the Blacksmith, the Squire and the Huntsman. Here a society lingers of people who are still down to earth, who know oats from barley, talk of heifers and geldings and can tell at a glance what a pig is worth. Folk from the suburbs have some lingering memory of what their grandmother told them, some story about haymaking or poaching. They long to lean on a gate and ask intelligent questions about lambing or cattle feed. They feel cut off from the countryside of their imagining and condemned to a life that is artificial and sterile. Their only consolation lies in the car, which will take them into the fields, through the woods, over the hills and far away. On the weekends, at least, they can be at one again with nature, countrymen all.

But the motor-car destroys what its driver comes to seek. The old market place was beautiful until it was filled with cars. Oxford chimes were romantic until the traffic made them inaudible. People used to paint watercolours of the Cathedral Close, but that was before they installed the parking meters. Crossing the road by the Guildhall has become rather a hazardous affair these days and the Castle is impossible to visit, there being nowhere to leave the car. No square retains its dignity when filled with radiators and number plates. No High Street remains picturesque when packed with vehicles, bumper to bumper. It is even a question whether the vibration of the passing trucks may not destroy the buildings altogether. As for the country, the cars parked at the beauty spots are themselves the blot on the landscape. The litter from a hundred picnics turns the loveliest river bank into a sort of slum. The moorland is marred by the traffic on the arterial road, the woods are noisy with the transistor radios which the cars have brought. Vehicles pack the village street and choke the entrance to the coaching Inn. Horses can scarcely venture on the road and petrol leaks put the hounds off the scent. In escaping from the dreary place where he lives, the motorist kills the place he has come to see. He brings with him not only death but destruction.

To save mankind from the motor-car is no easy task but to save any particular place is relatively easy. All the local authorities have to do is forbid the entrance of all mechanised vehicles, any that trespasses being liable to confiscation. The simplest resolution would thus save Cambridge or Keswick should it occur to anyone that they might be worth saving. The task is admittedly easier, however, when the place to be protected is an island. On Sark, for example, the law is admirably straightforward. 'No cars,' say the islanders and there are no cars. They have created, without difficulty, one of the few quiet places which remain in the British Isles. People come from all over the world to see and experience what Sark has to offer. If they are not prepared to walk, they have their choice between a horsedrawn vehicle and a bicycle. There is no similar law in Jersey, Guernsey or Alderney where cars are numerous, so that Sark is thus unique even among the Channel Islands. These differ in other respects so that the prospective visitor or resident should never say 'I am going to the Channel Islands' but must be specific. Each has something to offer which the others lack. What they have chiefly in common is the fascination which any island has for someone who wants to escape from the traffic and the noise, the dirt and the smog. For some people, moreover, an island is an end in itself.

In making comparison between Guernsey and Jersey, the intending resident must realise, first of all, that Jersey, the larger island, is almost without neighbours. Guernsey has its satellites, Sark and Herm, Jethou and Lihou, with

Alderney in the distance and Brechou a satellite of Sark. It is the Guernsey group, therefore, that has attracted the real island-lovers. These have ranged from the Blücher family (who quarrelled with Bismark and decided, therefore, to breed kangaroos in Herm) to Compton Mackenzie, once the monarch of Jethou; from the author of *Les Miserables* to the author of *Camelot*. Of all these individualists T. H. White was perhaps the most eccentric. I knew him first in Alderney, where much of his life was spent. It was our first choice among the islands and we were there in 1959, recuperating between two of our American campaigns. We were forced to conclude, in the end, however, that Alderney was more suitable for Tim White than it could ever be for us. And if Alderney was too small for our needs, Sark, as we realised, is smaller still. Guernsey thus became the inevitable base, with the other islands a frequent playground in summer. Each year has brought us to Sark and each visit has given us the excuse to call on the Dame, Mrs Sibyl Hathaway, by whose feudal court the island is governed.

Sibyl Hathaway is not to be classed among the islanders by choice, she being Dame of Sark by hereditary succession. Her family, the Collings of Guernsey, acquired the Lordship of Sark in 1852. The actual purchaser was Mrs T. G. Collings but she delegated the administration to her son, the Rev. W. T. Collings. He was the grandfather of the present Dame, who succeeded her father in 1926 and became Mrs Hathaway by her second marriage in 1929. Her husband died in 1954, since when she has been Dame and the island's effective ruler. Although the feudal system survives for some purposes in Jersey and Guernsey, the Courts being held and the dues being paid, the Sark Chief Pleas are unique in that no other administration exists in the island. In Sark the Seneschal can commit the offender to his own prison and he has his Prevot (Sheriff), Greffier (Clerk) and Constable (Tipstaff) to enforce the sentence. The legislature comprises forty members holding office by virtue of their freeholds and twelve deputies elected by the other less privileged inhabitants.

Sibyl Hathaway

Although the island is dependent upon Guernsey for some services, the Dame holds directly of the Sovereign, and her Court can do very much what it likes. Direct taxation there is none, divorce is not granted or recognised, and to possess or drive a motor-car (as distinct from a tractor) is a punishable offence. All these local peculiarities arise from the fact that the island is very much what its Seigneurs and Dames have made it. It thus remains triumphantly different and true to itself.

Sybil Hathaway is herself the symbol of Sark independence, a lady of tremendous personality. When the Channel Islands were 'demilitarised', all the population left Alderney and many inhabitants left Jersey and Guernsey. But the Hathaways stood their ground in Sark and nearly all their people resolved to do the same. When the Germans landed it was Sibyl Hathaway, at her most formidable, that they had to deal with. It was during the Occupation, in fact, that the Dame made her name for courage, wisdom and tact. Alone from the time of her husband's imprisonment in Germany, she never lost her nerve or her temper. She defied the Germans only on matters of principle, as when she agreed to circulate but refused to sign their orders. Steadfastly correct in her official business, she never allowed politeness to become collaboration. She took terrible risks in saving and concealing food for her people when they were all near starvation. It was she who faced the Germans when they landed. It was to her they surrendered when their regime collapsed. And now, when World War II is a thing of the past, hers is the legend which remains. To quote from her autobiography: 'Sark is not only the loveliest and least spoilt of the Channel Islands, it is unparalleled in so far as it has maintained the special privileges granted to it centuries ago. Just as long as my life may be extended, I shall strive to maintain this little feudal paradise with all its tradition, laws and customs, an oasis of quiet and rest, unique in the present-day world.' The quiet of Sark is the result of outlawing the car. Nor is this the modern application of some medieval law against vehicles costing more than a certain sum. The motor vehicle is not unknown in Sark; it has appeared there and has been rejected.

It all dates back, I find, to World War I, during which the Channel Islands were still garrisoned, after a fashion, and ready to defend themselves. Warlike preparations extended even to Sark, where an officer was stationed with a few men. With this party came a motor-cycle which roamed round the island giving a vivid preview of what a motorised Sark would be like. Nothing was done until the troops left but the Seigneur and his tenants had reached, meanwhile, a great decision. A law was passed prohibiting the import of any mechanically propelled vehicle without express permission and licence of the Chief Pleas; a licence which is never granted except in the case of tractors. For years these might be used only for agriculture but the privilege is now extended to cover the haulage of building materials. Even now, all tractors must be off the road by ten at night. Does the tractor represent the thin end of the wedge, a first step towards decline and fall? It would seem not. One car was actually imported by a new physician—on the plea, no doubt, that he could the sooner reach the scene of an emergency. Chief Pleas ordered the car off the island, and it went. More recently there was argument over the proposed importation of an ambulance, but here again the danger was averted. Who was to know what joy-riding might have been introduced under this specious pretext? The law is still upheld: being successfully infringed, however, by the Germans in World War II. They brought in not only lorries but *tanks!* When peace returned it was peace indeed, with cars forbidden and no transistor radios allowed on the cliffs and beach. Sark remains to this day among the quiet places of the world, its peace broken only by the sound of the horses' hooves.

The feudalism of Sark is tolerated as a picturesque survival, much as a ruined castle may be regarded as a tourist attraction. Feudalism as it survives in Jersey and Guernsey is sometimes criticised as a monstrous anachronism, contrary to the spirit of the age in which we live. Behind the trappings of feudalism lurk the memories (it is said) of injustice and privilege. But feudalism was never merely a system of tyranny. It provided, rather, a pattern of obligations and rights, with privilege balanced by duty and powers defined by law. The Dame of Sark has no absolute authority, nor can it be said that her predecessors had much more. What she has is an hereditary position of leadership with the right to encourage and the power to restrain. If this is an anomaly it is one which events have justified. Sark is not only prosperous but offers the sharpest contrast with an adjacent island where the hereditary system has been lost. Alderney was subject, in its happier days, to the leasehold governorship of a single family. Sir Edmund Andros acquired the lease by purchase from Lady Carteret, and left it to his nephew, George Andros. On his death in 1706, the lease went to George's sister, Anne, wife of John Le Mesurier, and the island was ruled by that family until 1825. The last hereditary governor surrendered his patent, says Edith Carey, 'in a fit of pique at the ingratitude of the people', but the last John Le Mesurier, a clergyman, built them their church in 1850. Since then the folk of Alderney have ruled themselves under the remote control of Guernsey. As compared with Sark, their regime has been uniformly disastrous, with little attempted and nothing achieved. 'The first impression on landing', wrote Edith Carey in 1904, 'is that of desolation and ruin.' That is the impression which remains today.

It could be argued that Sark has natural advantages which Alderney does not share. This is manifestly untrue, the wild aspect of the larger island being merely the result of neglect. As against that, the history of Alderney has been unfortunate, involving the replacement of its indigenous population. Swamped by its Victorian garrison and by the workmen imported to build its 19th-century fortifications and harbour, whatever remained of Alderney's local traditions went with the island's evacuation in 1940. But the crucial disaster was that of 1825, the Le Mesuriers' abandonment of their task. It is true that their lease would have expired in 1862 and might not have been renewed, but their continued association with the island might still have made all the difference. What a family can give, as in Sark, is a consistency of policy which extends beyond the span of a single lifetime. Beauty of landscape is seldom created or maintained by appointed officials or elected majorities. They cannot look sufficiently far ahead. If we are to judge feudalism and democracy by their effects rather than by our memories of the schoolroom, and if we are to regard Sark and Alderney as examples of what may result, the case for feudalism becomes unanswerable. The medieval institutions of Sark have been more than picturesque, they have been efficient, whereas the modern administration of Alderney has been insolvent as well as absurd.

What Alderney *can* offer is a suitable background for eccentric and colourful personalities. Such a character was Judge French, last survivor of an older regime, and victim of the revolt which drove him from office. Despite his local unpopularity, French remained in the island, where he earned a vast income by the writing of textbooks for colonial schools. It was he who told me the story of how the Alderney jetty came to have its crooked shape. There was fierce controversy at the time between two political groups, known respectively as the Judge's Party and the Cockroaches. A Commission heard the evidence of master mariners, fishermen, shipowners and pilots, some of whom said that the jetty should be crooked and others predicted disaster if it were other than straight; their evidence following the pattern of their political allegiance. French's predecessor in office won the day and the crooked jetty was the result. Such was the design, it transpired, that the Southern Railway steamship could not come alongside, the monopoly thus remaining with the local vessel of which the Judge happened to be owner. French's own period of office was made memorable

SYBIL HATHAWAY
T. H. WHITE

by his attempt to enforce the licensing laws, which were and are perpetually infringed. Having obtained all the necessary evidence, he put a test case to the Jurats, who were unanimous for acquittal and against whose verdict he could do nothing.

French was a recluse in his later years, shutting himself away from the people who had rejected his rule. All he did with his ample leisure was to build model boats which he finally gave away. All he did with his ample fortune was to leave it, mostly, to an English diocese. His was an example of wasted talent in a world where ability is all too scarce. The same could not be said of Tim White, a bachelor whose habits gave the islanders something to gossip about. Tim had once been a master at Stowe, where he taught English Literature. At about the age of thirty he realised that he would have to escape at once if he was not to remain a schoolmaster for the rest of his life. He fled to Alderney and settled down to a life of authorship. Tim's gifts ranged from oil painting to poetry, his knowledge from the Arthurian Cycle to the 18th century, his enthusiasms from falconry to amateur theatricals. His success as a teacher and novelist depended on his immaturity. Tim never rose beyond the 5th Form except in intellect. His sex and his humour were on the dormitory level, his emotions those felt by the schoolboy for the housemaster's daughter (or wife) and his fictional heroes resembled him by being merely boys in disguise. But these limitations did not prevent him from writing successfully. They were the secret, in fact, of the appeal he had to his public. A perpetual boyhood is easier to maintain, however, on paper than in life. Tim shrank from any adult relationship with either sex, taking refuge sometimes with the seabirds on the otherwise uninhabited island of Burhou, or else (and more tragically) taking refuge in the bottle. He had the bachelor's confidence where children are concerned, and once offered to adopt my son, Charles, whose parents, he felt, were unequal to the task of playing Merlin to Charles's Arthur. Our unvoiced objections to this plan included a doubt as to whether the ideal guardian should be alternately marooned on a rock or blind drunk in his studio.

We were in Alderney at the time when Tim sold the film rights in King Arthur. The purchasing syndicate had to charter an aircraft, on his insistence, to bring him to the conference, and the pilot had to circle seabird sanctuaries on the way. He was naturally elated at the idea of *Camelot* appearing on Broadway as the musical successor to *My Fair Lady*. His friends were more dubious, wondering whether sudden wealth would be the death of him. Rumour had it that he could make about £2,000 a week in royalties, and calculations were made as to how much brandy that sum would buy. But these fears proved groundless and there followed a brief period during which Tim White was to be seen in New York with white tie, tails and opera cloak. He was very properly devoted at this time to Julie Andrews, the heroine of the show, whose attractions included the essential one of being safely married to someone else. That she could see something in this elderly admirer is the proof of her quality—and his. Her personality was in fact the show's principal asset, for *Camelot* has little else to commend it, being utterly forgettable in both libretto and score. What it does represent is the sort of thing that Tim liked; an improbable romance in an impossible setting, with magical interventions and splendid costumes, plenty of stage effects, and the screamingly funny use of the historical anachronism. Tim must have loved every minute of it. One supposed, on hearing of the project, that Lerner and Loewe wanted to use the Arthurian theme and chose one author at random to save themselves from being sued by the rest. But there could have been no greater mistake. They remained all too loyal to Arthur's story as Tim had conceived it and the result was a Christmas Pantomime suitable for that 5th Form from which he could never quite escape.

In Tim's schooldays, and mine, the middle school form-room was always adorned with a sepia-tinted engraving or fly-blown photograph of the Parthenon, vaguely indicating the classical source to which we were to look for inspiration. It was against this background that Tim White died, being buried at Piraeus following his death on a Mediterranean cruise. He had been happy, one hopes, during the years of his last success. If he is remembered, however, it will be in Alderney, where his house remains as a sort of memorial. Its yellow door opens on a tiny village square, giving little hint of what lies beyond. The rambling house is very much, moreover, what one would expect, with its studio adapted from an outhouse. There he painted some pictures which have since, I believe, been sold. One of these, I recall, had been an indifferent portrait of some local worthy, picked up in Guernsey for a few shillings. Urged by some motive which must remain obscure, Tim repainted the clothes and background, putting the sitter into the uniform of the Confederate Navy and posing him against a fort of the period under heavy bombardment. It is a collector's item for whoever now possesses it. Beyond all the evidences of bachelor eccentricity, however, lie the more unexpected features of the property; a swimming pool and an open-air theatre; the ideal scene for the sort of cabaret he may have planned. Whatever the stories may be about this improbable garden in Alderney, they are less entertaining than another story, which may even be true. Two Jehovah's Witnesses knocked on the yellow door (so the legend goes) which Tim finally opened. Grey-headed and wildly bearded, his spectacles flashing as he swayed, the drunken author listened silently to some twaddle about Jehovah, ending with a muttered appeal for funds. The collecting box was pushed forward as the sorry tale came to an end, and Tim glared at the fools who had disturbed him, Then suddenly he came forward as if to make a donation. 'I AM JEHOVAH!!' he thundered, grabbing at the box, 'Give me the money!' According to the story, those Jehovah's Witnesses are running still.

It might be thought that there is too much of Tim White in this portrait of Sibyl Hathaway and so perhaps there is. But Tim, no less than the Dame of Sark, may serve to illustrate the conclusions with which this chapter and the book must end. First of these is that people of great ability —and I scarcely mention anyone whose ability was less than exceptional—do not emerge, as a rule, from the happiest background. No one subject for my portraiture had, I would suppose, an ideal upbringing or an unchequered career. Biographers are prone to attribute psychological instability to the stresses and strains of an unhappy childhood. However accurate or however misconceived that theory may be —and happiness is surely difficult to measure—the fact must remain that obstacles are there to surmount. So commonly is this done that we may doubt, finally, whether the supposed handicap may not be an advantage. So far as my own observation goes, I would conclude that ability, although hereditary, is improved by an early measure of adversity and improved again by a later measure of success.

My second conclusion must be that ability is less specialised than we are often tempted to suppose. As between the future graduates in Arts and Science there is a mental divergence (it would seem) from the outset. Among students of the Arts, by contrast, the same ability might be applied to almost any career. Of the people I have tried to portray no one would have failed to succeed, had it been necessary, in some other direction; the artist as engineer, the scholar as barrister, the soldier as archaeologist or the actor as priest. Within a broad field of intellectual and artistic effort, the same abilities will earn the same success. Some of my portraits are of people like Marylin Wailes who have done everything from painting to dancing, from horse-breaking to music, who are as much at home in the studio as on the stage, who pass without visible effort from the hunting field to the British Museum. She and my father, with Evan John Simpson, may typify the versatility of the true artist. Here were people whose imagination and energy could enliven any scene and strengthen any cause. The same could not be said without reservation of Eric Gill, who soon turned against the society he might have served. As variously gifted perhaps as any, Geoffrey Callender presents the contrast of someone whose whole energies came to bear on a single task. His achievement was thus the greater, his personality the less.

My third and last conclusion is that no real barrier exists between thought and action, between the philosophers and the kings. In the world of satire, as in *Patience* or *Tantivy Towers*, there is a chasm depicted between the Horse Guards and Bloomsbury, between Chelsea and the Shires. But the Gilbert and Sullivan man of action has clearly seen no action of any kind. In the more stirring days, by contrast, of World War II, the poets became soldiers and the real soldiers all but turned into poets. When the war ended the remaining leaders were, many of them, men of almost Elizabethan accomplishment. Lord Tedder had been, as General Horrocks became, a student of history. Lord Wavell was editor of an anthology. Admiral Sir Charles Lambe would talk of Picasso while everyone knew that his real passion was for classical music. Among the best of these was Sir Gerald Templer, statesman as well as soldier, scholar as well as wit. In the same tradition was Richard Miers, whose eager mind ranged far beyond the battlefield and whose pen was as ready as his sword. Born to rule her tiny kingdom, Sibyl Hathaway has lived dangerously and yet written a better book than some whose pretensions are greater and whose experience is less.

Matching the ease with which the born leaders turn to literature or art is the skill which the best artists display in business or war. Edward Welbourne had earned a military reputation before he had proved himself in scholarship or administration. Arthur Bryant was destined, like Welbourne, for the Bar, and who would question that either would have ended on the Bench? Considering all these careers afresh we might well reach the conclusion that the man of thought is no more than the man to whom action has been denied. 'Every man,' said Dr Johnson, 'thinks meanly of himself for never having been a soldier or never having gone to sea.' In the generation with which this book is concerned there are authors and artists who have seen action and are the better men in consequence. How many, however, would write if they had been allowed to govern, how many would paint if they had been given the chance to lead?

Looking back on the period through which these characters lived, and considering the world into which many of them have survived, we note an apparent change in the qualities which now give access to the corridors of power. Office goes increasingly to the politician who has studied nothing but politics. Mr Lee Kuan Yew thus typifies the man of the future, a Far Eastern Wilson or Maudling, as remote from the studio as the battlefield, as different from Sir Winston Churchill as anyone could be. Under this new type of ruler, the graduate in politics and economics, the one thing certain is that the men of action must join the men of thought in oblivion. There has never been an age when either group has mattered less or when bureaucracy has mattered more. I have been writing, in effect, about men and women whose world is finished. They could not save the society into which they had been born. It remains to their credit that they tried.

INDEX

৯৫৯

Index

Index

Lanteri, Professor, 5
'Lee, Jane', *see* Ann Parkinson
Lee Kuan Yew, 133, 136–7, 139–44, 176
Le Mesurier, Anne (*née* Andros), 169; John (1706), 169; Rev. John (1850), 169–70
Lennox-Boyd, Alan (Viscount Boyd of Merton), 137
Lerner, Jay, 172
Lim Yew Hock, 138
Lincoln, Abraham, 154–5
Liverpool Cathedral, 95–7
Llanfoist, Vicar of, 14
Loewe, Arthur, 172
London Regiment, 22nd, 60–1

Macaulay, William, 51
MacDonald, Ramsay, 41, 58
MacGillivray, Sir Donald, 122, 125
Mackenzie, Sir Compton, 166
Macmillan Commission, 45
Macpherson, The, 57
Malaya, 118, 120–2, 126–7, 129–31; Arts Theatre Group, 126; Forum Club, 126; Independence celebrations, 130; Kuala Trengganu Rest House, 130; Kuala Lumpur, 123; National Museum, 126; National Parks, 126; St John's Ambulance, 124; T.B. Research Hospital, 124; Women's Institutes, 124; University of, 117, 131; University Archaeological Society, 131
Malayan Civil Service, 121, 122–4
Malayan Sunday Times, 139
Manchester Guardian, 130
Marlborough School, 85
Marshall, David, 135–8, 141; Prof. Alfred, 42–3, 47
Marston Moor, Battle of, 19
Marx, Karl, 43
Masefield, John, 19, 26–7
Mends, Brig.-Gen., 23
Miers, Charles, 151; James (Richard's brother), 148–9, 151–2; Brig. Richard, 146–52, 155–8, 175; Sue (Mrs Richard), 147, 150, 154, 156
Milne, A. A., 81–2
Ming Lee, 153

Montgomery of Alamein, Field-Marshal Viscount, 119, 124
Morris, William, 8–9, 92
Morton, Dorothy (Dorothy Wailes-Fairbairn), *see* Wailes
Muir, Ramsay, 42

Napoleon, 102
National Trust, 94
Nelson, Lord, 103, 109, 124
New College, Oxford, 88
New Statesman, The, 40
Newton, Prof. A. P., 57–8
Nicolson, Sir Harold, xi
Noah's Ark Touring Company, 20, 22–3
Northcote family, 4
Nye, Lt.-Gen. Sir A., 119

Offler, Prof. H. S., 38
Osborne, Royal Naval College, 89
Ospovat, Henry, 9

Palmerston, Lord, 73
Parkinson, Ann (Mrs C. Northcote Parkinson), 126, 139, 141, 146, 150, 155, 159; Charles, 171; The Rev. R. C., xiii, 1–2, 4, 6, 7, 17, 27, 33, 55, 64; Mrs W. E. (*née* Rose Emily Mary (Rosemary) Curnow), 4, 6, 10, 13–14, 16–18, 21–2, 26, 61; William Edward, 1–11, 13–15, 17–18, 21, 27, 30, 59, 174
Parkinson's Law (C. Northcote Parkinson), 127, 129–30
Parrish, Maxfield, 9
Pearson, Martin, 23
Pellew, Edward, *see* Exmouth
Penn, William, 29
Pepys, Samuel, 109–10
Pétain, Marshal, 28
Picasso, Pablo, 175
Pigou, Prof. A. C., 43
Popham, Lord Chief Justice, 94
Public Record Office, 56, 85

Raffles, Sir Stamford, 132
Ramsden, Omar, 9
Reade, Charles, 72
Rhodes, K. H., 18

179

Index